DIVING INTO DARKNESS
The Elements of Safe Night Diving

DIVING INTO DARKNESS
The Elements of Safe Night Diving

Robert N. Rossier

BEST PUBLISHING COMPANY

ISBN: 0-941332-94-2
Library of Congress catalog card number: 00-109192

Best Publishing Company
2355 North Steves Boulevard
P.O. Box 30100
Flagstaff, Arizona 86003-0100 USA

For Bonnie

Table of Contents

Chapter 4: Human Factors and the Night Diver

Chapter 5: Night Diving Planning and Procedures

Foreword

Night diving is pretty much as Forest Gump describes life—like a box of chocolates. The darkness has a sweet allure, we never know what we'll find, and the mystery is tantalizing. Even when daytime dives become plain vanilla, every night dive is rich, dark, and different. Leafing through my logbook, which spans some 25 years, I can't help but note the differences in each night dive. I call it the late show—sitting on the bottom with my light off watching the twinkling trail of bioluminescence that follows every move, every bubble. Sneaking up on a sleeping bass. Gaping at a twisted tangle of spider crabs forming a living carpet on the sea floor. Having the silver streak of a six-foot tarpon suddenly shoot through the beam of my light. No two dives are the same at night. Beyond the differences I've discovered in night diving experiences, I'm struck by the advances in the technology, techniques, and training that make night diving now more pleasurable and safer than ever.

There's much more to night diving than simply flipping the switch on a new, high-tech dive light. The night environment, like any other new dive environment, demands the requisite knowledge, skills, and experience to be accomplished with safety. The purpose of this book is to lay out in a logical and thorough manner the many factors that separate day diving from night, and outline the procedures used to make night diving as safe as possible.

When the sun sets, we don our gear to open that box of chocolates and contemplate its dark mysteries. The only way to believe what is out there is to see it with your own eyes. Get the right equipment and training to go with it, and you've got your ticket to the late show.

R.N. Rossier

Acknowledgments

It's always impressive to get to the end of a book-writing project and tally up all the individuals who contributed to the effort. In a way, it's odd that only the author's name gets printed on the cover. So many people make significant contributions, and they deserve much more credit than they ever receive. Without their efforts and expertise, a project like this would be impossible. I would like to extend personal thanks and recognition to:

Dr. Mel Cundiff of the University of Colorado in Boulder for his extensive inputs and insights into night marine biology;
Dr. Glen Egstrom who shared his insights into the human factors considerations of diving;
Dr. Hillary Viders, who provided insights into human performance and night diving emergencies;
Scott Mele of Tektite for his assistance and technical review of the section on dive lights; and
Steve Barnett, Dr. Mel Cundiff, and Jeff Hewlett for their excellent photographs.

Numerous individuals also provided technical assistance and acted as sounding boards as I sifted through the information to be provided in this book. Among these were Alex Brylske, technical editor for *Dive Training* magazine; Cathryn Castle, editor of *Dive Training* magazine; Fred Fisher of Underwater Kinetics; Dee Scarr, noted naturalist and lecturer; David Swain, instructor and owner of Ocean State Scuba in Jamestown, RI; and Mark Young, publisher of *Dive Training* magazine.

I could never have managed to complete this project had it not been for the love, patience, and encouragement of my wife, Lori. Also essential to the project were my children, Rachel and Ethan, who provided comic relief and helped "field test" a number of the dive lights.

Finally, special thanks to Jim Joiner of Best Publishing Company who edited the final manuscript, and his fine staff who put it all together.

While I'm deeply indebted to all these individuals, the content of this book including any errors and omissions are entirely my responsibility.

Disclaimer

Scuba diving involves inherent risks that must be accepted by any individual engaging in the sport. Neither the author nor the publisher accept responsibility for accidents or injuries resulting from the use of materials contained herein. The information in this book should be considered a supplement to an approved night diving training program provided by a nationally recognized scuba certification agency. This book cannot take the place of training provided by a professional instructor. All certified divers should receive professional instruction and certification in night diving before attempting to dive in darkness.

In addition to the information contained herein, all divers should follow the safe diving rules, practices, and procedures taught at every level of scuba certification. Professional training, certification, routine review of diving skills and knowledge, and adherence to conservative diving practices and procedures are necessary ingredients for safe recreational diving.

Other Books by the Author:

Dive Like a Pro: 101 Ways to Improve Your Diving Skills and Safety

Exploring Diving: The Diver's Guide to Underwater Training and Adventure

Recreational Nitrox Diving

For more information contact:

Best Publishing Company
2355 North Steves Boulevard
P.O. Box 30100
Flagstaff, AZ 86003-0100
Email: divebooks@bestpub.com
Fax: 520.526.0370
Phone: 800.468.1055 or 520.527.1055

CHAPTER 1

Into the Darkness:
An Introduction to Night Diving

1.1 Why Night Dive?

Just ask anyone who has made a dive at night, and they're bound to tell you it's among the best and most exciting dives they've ever done. There must be at least a hundred good reasons to dive at night. Night diving offers a whole new perspective on diving and on the underwater world. Even a familiar daytime dive site is transformed by darkness. Viewed in the illuminating beam of a dive light, the bottom comes alive with new and interesting life, and explodes in rich and vibrant colors.

FIGURE 1-1 *(S.M. Barnett)*
Divers explore the wreck of the *Doc Paulsen* at night.

Even if you're familiar with the aquatic or marine creatures in your favorite underwater haunt, you may be surprised to see them engaged in different activities. Fish seldom seen except for a brief glimpse can be approached and studied as they sleep. Other nocturnal marvels of nature are out and about, searching for food, and the darkness creates a stunning black backdrop to photographs. The opportunities for finding, observing and photographing marine and aquatic life is a strong lure for many divers.

While the diurnal migration of plankton can reduce nighttime visibility in many areas of the ocean, other areas may actually have better visibility at night. Once the sun goes down, the differential heating of the land and sea ceases. The winds die down, and the seas begin to calm, reducing the turbulent mixing that often spoils visibility.

Night diving offers a way to stay active in the sport while meeting the demands of an otherwise busy schedule. For many people, daytime is work time, and evenings are reserved for recreation and physical activities. Night diving offers a great opportunity to practice your skills, get some exercise, and relax. Sharing an occasional evening with some friends on a local night dive can be fun as well as rejuvenating, but along with the thrill comes a need to maintain a high level of situational awareness, and to evaluate the continually changing environment.

1.2 Aquatic Decision Making and the Elements of Night Diving

At the core of our ability to dive safely is our judgment and decision-making ability. To exercise good judgment and make safe aquatic decisions requires a continuous assessment of three critical elements—the environment, our equipment, and our own abilities and limits—and each of these elements takes on new dimensions as daylight fades and shadows grow longer. Training and experience are vital factors in assessing these elements, but our experience and training in daytime diving does not necessarily prepare us for a night excursion under the waves.

1.2.1 Environment

Water conditions and diving environments considered well within our abilities for a day dive become much more difficult to negotiate at night. Even if we dive the exact same location at day and night, the environments for the two dives are vastly different.

Into the Darkness—An Introduction to Night Diving

The first reason is due to the reduced field of vision. While the water might actually be clearer at night than in the day, the fact that we can only see the area illuminated by our dive light has serious implications.

Often times, entanglement hazards readily seen during the day remain invisible at night. For this reason, it's important to carefully survey a dive site in the daylight before attempting a night dive. Divers must also learn to carefully scan the area around them with their dive light to reveal entanglement hazards that may not have been identified earlier.

At night, communications between divers takes on a new dimension. While the same hand signals used in daytime diving are often used at night, it may be necessary to illuminate our signing hand with our dive light so our buddy can see our signal. Alternatively, lights themselves are often used by night divers to communicate some signals such as "danger" and "okay."

Navigation, and in particular natural navigation, is some-times more difficult at night. Unless a landmark appears in the beam of our dive light, we might miss it entirely. On the other hand, strobes and other specialized lights are often used on the surface and below the waves to make night navigation easier than during the day.

While buddy contact is critical to safety on any dive, it's especially important on a night dive where problems are less likely to be noticed, and are more stressful and difficult to resolve. However, many divers find it easier to keep track of their buddy due to the fact that a buddy's light beam can easily be monitored even in the peripheral vision.

There's no doubt that equipment problems are more stress-ful and often harder to resolve on a night dive than during the day. It's generally more difficult to see a problem at night, the need to use a light can make resolving a problem awkward, and light failures can leave us in darkness until a backup light is located and turned on, or our eyes adjust to the available natural lighting.

1.2.2 Equipment

Our familiarity with our equipment becomes more critical when diving in darkness, and additional equipment is needed to ensure proper vision, communication, and navigation both underwater and on the surface.

The most obvious piece of equipment needed beyond our daytime dive equipment is a dive light. In fact, a night dive usually requires an array of lights used for various purposes. Besides a primary and backup light for the dive itself, divers often set up lights on the surface by which their equipment can be set up and donned. Divers may also wear identification lights, instrumentation lights, and emergency lights. Additional surface lights may be needed for navigational reference. Likewise, strobes and marker lights are frequently used to aid in locating the anchor line, down line, or for other navigational purposes.

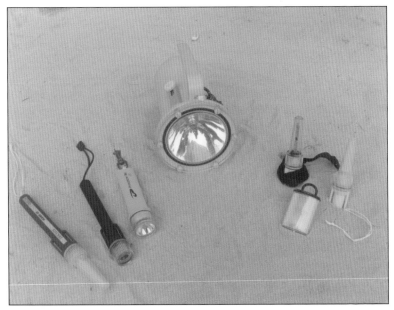

FIGURE 1-2 *(R.N. Rossier)*
A night dive usually requires an array of lights used for various purposes.

Into the Darkness—An Introduction to Night Diving

Since descents and ascents are more difficult at night, divers are encouraged to carry line reels, ascent lines, and lift bags in order to make open water or emergency ascents. The proper use of this equipment requires additional training and practice.

A few minor modifications to your regular equipment can better prepare you for the night diving environment. Clear identification tags or markings can help keep your gear together when gearing up in limited-light conditions. Additional clips and D-ring may be needed to accommodate lights, line reels, and lift bags. Reflective elements added to equipment eases diver identification on the surface and below.

1.2.3 Diver
Our own abilities and limits vary much like the daily cycles of day and night. Three major factors affect the diver, altering his performance on a night dive. The first is a psychological change, primarily in the form of increased stress associated with entering the underwater environment in darkness.

Next are physiological changes in a diver a night. With the psychological stress come a narrowing of visual perception, and an increase in breathing rate, both of which affect the diver's performance. Night divers may also face challenges in terms of fatigue and nutritional shortcomings, which can degrade their performance.

Finally, biomechanical limitations may affect the diver's performance on a night dive. The need to manipulate a dive light may leave a diver only one hand to contend with routine tasks as well as with minor equipment problems and emergencies that can develop on any dive.

1.3 Night Diver Training
Those three primary elements of aquatic decision making—environment, equipment, and the diver himself—offer a significant challenge to any diver who ventures beneath the waves at night. To a great extent, the challenges can be overcome through training. While night diver training includes a myriad of

skills and drills, perhaps the most important elements that allow us to overcome the challenges of night diving are the tools and techniques we use to plan our dives, and the procedures used to safely execute that plan. As part of night diver specialty training, divers learn how to assess the environment, their equipment and themselves in relation to the demands of night diving.

The following chapters provide an in-depth look at the night diving environment, the equipment used, and us as divers. We'll also examine the detailed planning and procedures that result in safe enjoyable night diving.

CHAPTER 2

The Night Diving Environment

2.1 More Than Darkness

The night diving environment means more than just darkness. When the sun goes down, many factors come into play that make the process of diving more challenging. Certainly, when the primary source of illumination is from our dive light, our field of vision is restricted. But other considerations, such as the diurnal migration of zooplankton, can affect the visibility on a night dive. In this chapter, we'll consider water movement, weather, and changes in marine life activity as the three main environmental elements in night diving.

FIGURE 2-1 *(R.N. Rossier)*
Many factors come into play to make diving more challenging when the sun goes down.

2.2 The Ocean in Motion

It's almost impossible to consider a dive without considering the potential effects of currents, surf, and surge. While a small

lake or pond may have virtually none of these dynamic characteristics, most open water dive sites do, and their effect on us
can be more difficult to detect in the restricted visual field of a
night dive. Even a gentle current can move us far enough during the course of a half-hour dive to seriously compromise our
navigation at the surface. Strong surf and surge is not only dis-
orienting in shallow water, it can make entries and exits more
hazardous, particularly in areas where footing can be tenuous.
For this reason, night divers should consider these factors quite
carefully. In general, night dives should be avoided in conditions
of currents and strong surf or surge.

Entanglement hazards pose a serious threat, especially in
moving water. Potential underwater snares such as fishing lines,
nets, and submerged wreckage and tree branches may be less
easily detected at night due to our limited visual field. Dive sites
should be surveyed in the daylight to identify such hazards. If
serious entanglement hazards exist, consider changing the dive
location.

2.3 Marine Weather

Weather conditions play an important role on a night dive,
so make a careful check of weather before heading out.
Remember, too, that approaching weather systems are less
likely to be seen at night, so the weather check is even more
important than on daytime dives. In this section, we'll take a
closer look at some of the more troublesome weather phenomenon, the conditions that cause them, and sources of marine
weather information.

2.3.1 Frontal Weather Phenomenon

Of particular importance to the weather is atmospheric stability. High humidity translates to low stability. Under the right
conditions, unstable conditions set the stage for showers, fog,
and thunderstorms, all of which can impact our diving plans,
especially at night.

What often initiates the onset of bad weather is an
approaching front. Fronts are loosely defined as boundaries
between air masses of differing temperatures, or areas of

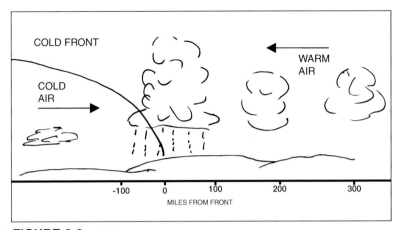

FIGURE 2-2
As a cold front is wedged under warm, moist, unstable air, cumulus clouds with showers and thunderstorms are likely to develop near the surface position of the front. Convective clouds form ahead of the front, and moisture laden air forms fair weather cumulus clouds in the cold air behind the front.

different climatological conditions. The weather typically associated with fronts includes not only changes in temperature, but shifting winds, and often times precipitation. In fact, the most severe weather phenomena are associated with frontal zones.

Of particular interest are cold fronts which occur when masses of colder air move through an area replacing warmer air. In the northern hemisphere, cold air masses form in the north, and generally move from northwest to southeast. The approach of a cold front is signaled by a drop in barometric pressure, and is followed by a rise in pressure following the frontal passage. Interestingly enough, the nasty weather can arrive well before the front itself. The cold air drives underneath the warm air like a wedge, (see FIGURE 2-2) pushing the warm air upward. As the air rises, it cools, moisture in the air condenses, and clouds form. This can mean something as innocuous as showery weather, or as dangerous as the development of severe showers and thunderstorms.

9

The severity of weather preceding a cold front passage is to a large degree a function of the speed at which the front is moving. The faster the front moves, the more sever the weather. The same is true for temperature. When surface temperature differences exceeding 8°F occur within 50 miles of the front, expect gusty winds and generally rough conditions associated with the frontal movement.

2.3.2 Thunderstorms

One of the most prevalent and spectacular forms of severe weather is the thunderstorm, and this is one weather phenomenon to avoid entirely when planning a night dive. Each year, over a hundred thousand thunderstorms sweep across the U.S. alone, with over 1,800 thunderstorms occurring worldwide in the atmosphere every hour. While the natural beauty of thunderstorms often entrances us, we should never grow complacent regarding their true danger. The energy of a single lightning bolt, according to one source, can be 15 to 30 million volts at 100,000 amps, and can reach temperatures of 50,000°F. Some 90 deaths and 300 personal injuries are attributed to lightning each year.

Lightning is only one of the hazards associated with thunderstorms. In addition to the blinding discharges capable of frying a boat and its crew, a single major thunderstorm may involve more energy than a nuclear bomb. Thunderstorms can generate destructive turbulence, torrential rain, pummeling hail, and hundred-mile-an-hour winds that whip the seas into a maelstrom. While most boaters are savvy enough to avoid areas of thunderstorm activity during the day, remember that it can be particularly difficult at night to detect the development of towering cumulus clouds that lead to thunderstorms. Moreover, it can be difficult if not impossible to outrun an approaching thunderstorm at night. The effects of thunderstorms extend far beyond their physical limits. Damaging hail can be spit out some twenty miles beyond cumulonimbus clouds, thunderstorms, and their anvils. Gusty, turbulent winds can occur within 20 miles of a major thunderstorm, and within 10 miles of less severe storms.

Even without radar, you can make a crude approximation of the distance of a thunderstorm. To estimate the distance in miles between you and a thunderstorm, divide the time interval between the flash and the thunderclap in seconds by five. A ten-second interval means the storm is two miles away. Static on an AM radio is another good sign that thunderstorms are near.

If thunderstorms are forecast at night, it's best to plan your diving for another night. Thunderstorm watches and warnings are broadcast over NOAA weather radio. Those who choose to ignore thunderstorm warnings are often surprised and over-come by the severity of the conditions.

2.3.3 Fog

Another potential weather problem for night diving is fog. Fog can make it virtually impossible to navigate back to port or shore without the aid of radar or electronic navigation. Fog occurs when the air becomes saturated with water vapor. Since warm air can hold more moisture than cool air, any time the air temperature cools to the dew point (saturation point), fog will form.

Several types of fog can be a problem for divers and boaters. The first is radiation fog, or ground fog, which occurs on clear, still nights when the land radiates energy back to space, cooling the overlying air to the dew point. Usually this type of fog will burn off with the return of the sun's heat (little help for night divers), or dissipate when winds develop and mix up the still air. Similarly, steam fog occurs when warm ocean or lake waters evaporate into cooler overlying air. Steam fog is relatively unsta-ble, and can quickly form and dissipate. Another form of fog is called advection fog, and it develops when warm, moist air moves over cooler coastal waters (or colder land), cooling the air to the dew point and forming a dense blanket of fog. Finally, precipitation fog occurs when warm rain falls through cool air, and is often associated with frontal activity.

The key to fog formation is the temperature-dew point spread. Any time the spread decreases to 5°F or less, conditions are favorable for fog formation.

11

FIGURE 2-3   *(R.N. Rossier)*
Fog can make it virtually impossible to navigate back to port or shore.

2.3.4 Wind, Seas, and Swell

Another important consideration for any night dive, whether from shore or a boat, is the sea conditions. Large waves can make boat diving uncomfortable, if not dangerous, and heavy, pounding surf can pose problems for beach entries and exits, especially when negotiating the shoreline in darkness.

An important distinction is the difference between sea and swell. The "seas" are wind-driven waves, and their size is a function of the wind velocity, the duration for which the wind has been blowing, and the "fetch" or distance over which the wind has been blowing. Swells are a product of past wind conditions, and are often larger than the prevailing wind-driven seas. More importantly, swells can come from an entirely different direction than the seas, causing particularly uncomfortable and rough conditions.

Even if our forecasts lack expected sea conditions, wind forecasts can give us a good clue as to what might be expected. Small craft advisories are posted when winds are

12

forecasted from 18 to 33 knots. Winds in the 17 to 21 knot range can generate seas of 4 to 8 feet, while winds in the 28 to 33 knot range can generate 13 to 20 foot seas in open water. As these waves approach shallow water, the waves will increase in height (with a corresponding decrease in wavelength), becoming even more dangerous. Gale warnings (winds 34 to 47 knots) can tear the tops off waves, reducing visibility in heavy spray. Tropical storms warnings (48 to 63 knot winds) and Hurricane warnings (more than 64 knots) can whip the seas to heights of 20 to 45 feet or more, with overhanging wave crests in open waters.

Remember, too, that depth gradients and shoreline contours can significantly affect the size of waves as they approach shore. As waves enter shallow water, the bottom of the wave begins to "drag" on the seafloor, slowing down the bottom of the wave and shortening the wavelength. As the wavelength decreases, the wave is "compressed" and increases in height. When a critical proportion of height to wavelength is reached, the wave breaks.

As a wave approaches shore at an angle, the slowing effect as the wave drags on the bottom tends to turn the wave parallel to shore. The faster part of the wave (further from shore) effectively catches up with the slower part (closer to shore). So as waves approach a point of land, they build in height and turn parallel to shore, focusing their energy and potentially destructive force on the point.

While these same phenomena occur day and night, the

TABLE 2-1 Wind Speed and Wave Height Ranges for Marine Weather Forecasts

Warning Condition	Wind Speed (knots)	Open Water Wave Height (feet)
Small Craft Warning	17–21	4–8
Small Craft Warning	28–33	13–20
Gale Warning	34–47	20 plus
Tropical Storm Warning	48–63	20 to 45 plus
Hurricane Warning	64 and higher	20 to 45 plus

FIGURE 2-4
Waves build in height and turn parallel to shore as they approach a point of land.

(R.N. Rossier)

effects are more difficult to see at night. For this reason, it can be important to observe the dive site in daylight hours and note the interaction of the shoreline and sea conditions.

2.3.5 Tides and Currents

Tides and currents are another important part of the night diving weather picture. Tides often affect the underwater visibility, as well as determine the strength and direction of currents. The times for high and low tides are broadcast via NOAA VHF weather forecasts, and are often found in local newspapers. Marine supply stores usually sell nautical almanacs that provide information on tides and currents.

14

Rip tides and longshore currents often spell danger, particularly at night when divers are less apt to notice their affects. Many nautical almanacs contain information on local currents, and the professionals at local dive centers may also be able to steer you clear of such hazards.

2.3.6 Water Temperature

Even if the weather conditions are favorable for a night dive, temperatures tend to be lower at night, so heat loss is generally greater than on a daytime dive. Reduced body temperature translates to increased air consumption and a predisposition to DCS. If left unchecked, it can also lead to reduced mental acuity and reduced manual dexterity, both of which can lead to unsafe situations in the water (see CHAPTER 4). For these reasons, divers are encouraged to limit cold exposure on days when night diving is planned. Since the beam of our dive light narrows our focus, we tend to swim less on a night dive, and spend more time observing a smaller area. Consequently, we may tend to get colder on a night dive. So even in warm conditions, some form of exposure suit should be worn to limit heat loss.

2.3.7 Weather Reports and Forecasts

Just as important as understanding the basics of weather is knowing where to get current weather information. Numerous sources are available, depending on your location, and all can be used to develop a big weather picture for a night dive.

The weather channel is found on virtually every cable channel in the U.S., and it provides basic local and national weather information. Local papers and television networks also provide marine forecasts as part of their standard weather forecast in many coastal areas.

For more detailed information on sea conditions, the potential for fog, and other conditions of concern to boating and diving, consult the National Oceanic and Atmospheric Administration (NOAA) marine weather broadcasts. These pre-recorded forecasts, updated every one to three hours, are broadcast 24 hours a day on VHF frequencies of 162.400,

162.475, and 162.55 MHz. Inexpensive, portable VHF weather radios are available through discount department stores and other sources, and can be used to receive these broadcasts. Special storm warnings issued by the National Weather Service (NWS) are also broadcast over Coast Guard VHF Channel 22A (157.1 MHz).

Numerous sources of weather information can be found on the Internet. Many Internet service providers (ISP's) and search engines provide easy assess to weather information adequate for many planning purposes. Most list weather city by city, providing current weather conditions and extended forecasts. Some also include coastal and marine forecasts. One popular source is The Weather Channel's web site at www.weather.com.

For detailed weather information, it's tough to beat the National Weather Service (NWS) site at www.nws.noaa.gov. Here you'll gain access to various weather warnings, public forecasts, current conditions, weather maps, storm predictions, satellite images, marine weather and extended forecasts. Information is available for U.S. as well as international locations.

One particularly useful feature on the NWS site is access to the National Buoy Data Center. Here you can click up virtually any ocean buoy and coastal marine automated network (C-MAN) station and get real time weather data that's particularly helpful when planning a dive. Information typically includes water temperature, wind direction and speed, wind gusts, wave height, dominant wave period, and atmospheric pressure. Current data and historical data for the previous 12 hours is generally available.

2.4 The Night Shift: Marine Life at Night
Perhaps the most notable difference between day and night diving is the marine life, and this is often what draws a diver to night diving. Regardless of what type of waters you dive at night, you're certain to note differences in the behavior and activity of creatures living beneath the waves. In virtually any lake or pond,

fish seldom seen except at a glance can be approached as they sleep at night. In waters off the northeast, expect to find everything from bioluminescent dinoflagellates that glow with every flick of a fin, to armies of crustaceans prowling the bottom. You may never see a horn shark while diving in a West Coast kelp forest in the daylight, but these slow, odd-looking creatures will be seen at night scouring the bottom in search of crustaceans and sea urchins.

While the night life varies no matter where you dive, few places will have such a dramatic day/night shift as the coral reefs. During the daytime, the coral reef appears to be a bee-hive of activity with something happening everywhere all around us. At night, the focus of our attention shifts to the narrow beam of our dive light, and we find ourselves paying more attention to the smaller details often overlooked during the day. Zero in on the bright reflections of tiny eyes as you shine your light on the reef, and you'll find small shrimp staring back at you. While they're all there during the day, the reef seems to come alive with small, almost invisible creatures including nudibranchs, flatworms and those tiny shrimp. If the reef appears colorful in the daylight, at night the colors are even more brilliant due to the broad-spectrum intensity of our dive lights.

These are just some of the differences you'll note on a night dive, but in fact, the night life on a coral reef is worlds apart from the daytime activity, and the changes are seen across the entire spectrum of life from the tiniest plankton to the top apex predators. As diving naturalist and author Dee Scarr writes, "Night diving enables us to get a fuller understanding of the ebb and flow of life on the reef, because we're able to see activities that simply don't take place in the daytime."

While the most exciting organisms are found on the coral reef at night, virtually nothing found on the reef is aggressive to a diver. In fact, the biggest danger is often inadvertent contact with a long-needle sea urchin due to a diver's poor buoyancy control. Proper buoyancy control is essential to safe night diving.

Diving into Darkness

The differences in marine life observed at night begin at the most basic level. Phytoplankton (tiny, floating plants) stay in the surface waters of the ocean all the time, but are too small for us to see. The larger zooplankton (tiny animals) make a diurnal migration from depths of hundreds of feet deep where they spend their daylight hours to the surface waters each night to feed on the phytoplankton. Then with the coming of daylight, they return again to the depths. Most numerous of the zoo-plankton are the copepods. In fact, these are considered to be the most numerous macroscopic animals on earth ranging in size from 1/16" to 3/4" long with an estimated population density of three thousand per cubic meter of seawater in the upper waters. While the most strange-looking are larval forms of various crustaceans, such as crabs and lobsters, the most animated are planktonic annelids (segmented worms). To get a good idea of the numbers of these tiny creatures, try hanging a dive light off a boat late at night. The light will attract a splendid array of planktonic species, along with species such as mantas which feed on them.

Of course, jellyfish are part of the diurnally migrating plankton and tend to be in the surface waters at night. (Planktonic species are weak swimmers at the mercy of the currents, but not all of them are small!) Using an underwater light in the dark water actually makes it easier to see jellyfish at night than during the day. Since many jellyfish can cause stinging injuries, divers are encouraged to wear some form of protective garment (diveskin, wet suit, etc.) on a night dive. Keep your eyes wide open and avoid contact, especially in the face.

Although many ctenophores, or comb jellies, can be seen in daylight hours, others tend to be diurnal migrators, and thus are more likely to be seen in the surface waters at night. Some are bioluminescent, so if seen in the deeper, darker waters, this bioluminescence might be observed.

The arrival of the zooplankton sets in motion the entire activity of the underwater world. Many of the lower order reef inhabitants are filter feeders, and those which focus their feeding on the zooplankton can be decidedly more active and interesting at night. While sponges partaking in the evening feed generally look the same day or night, they may appear to be more colorful because of the bright, unfiltered light.

When we think of the coral reef, we first think of the corals that build the basic reef structure. Corals have a symbiotic relationship with zooanthellae (mostly species of dinoflagellates), who pay high rent in the form of glucose, but the primary source of nitrogen and nutrients for hard corals are the copepods that arrive as part of the nightly diurnal zooplankton migration. Corals "flower" or extend their polyps in order to capture their prey using their stinging cells (nematocysts or cnidocysts) on their tentacles. A few of the hard corals (*Phylum Cnidaria, Class Anthozoa*) such as finger corals and pillar corals flower all day long, thus creating a fuzzy appearance day and night. However, most hard corals only flower at night. Some species flower very slowly, and their polyps won't be fully extended until 9 or 10 p.m.—long after many divers have finished their night dive.

A particularly rare and fascinating scene witnessed by few fortunate divers is the "smoking" coral, where under the cover of darkness, corals spew forth their tiny egg sacks and sperm in synchronicity with the lunar cycle. This mass spawning occurs at different times throughout the world's oceans, but in each locale, the event is closely choreographed.

The appearance of soft corals doesn't vary appreciably between day and night since their polyps are out all the time. Gorgonians (one form of soft corals) tend not to change daily either, but broccoli corals (alcyonians), which are normally in a deflated state, tend to inflate with water during times of tidal currents. These currents are tied to the lunar cycle—not the daily (solar) cycle of day and night. However, the various starfish that populate stands of gorgonians can be a sight to behold at night.

Divers on the coral reef relatively rarely notice various flatworms (*Phylum Platyhelminthes*). It is likely that these tiny creatures are out and active all the time, but their bright colors are more evident in a night diver's bright lights, and for this reason they may be seen more often at night. Annelids, or

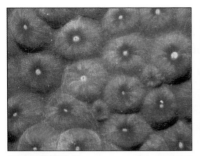

FIGURE 2-5 *(M. Cundiff)*
Boulder coral closed in daylight.

FIGURE 2-6 *(M. Cundiff)*
Boulder coral open at night.

FIGURE 2-7 *(S.M. Barnett)*
Orange cup corals feeding at night.

FIGURE 2-8 *(S.M. Barnett)*
A file clam opens at night.

FIGURE 2-9 *(S.M. Barnett)*
A spiny lobster hunts at night.

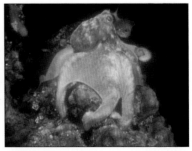

FIGURE 2-10 *(S.M. Barnett)*
An octopus hunts on the reef at night.

segmented worms such as Christmas tree worms, feather dusters, and bristleworms (fire worms) are seen both day and night, but the spaghetti worms are more active at night. If their long, sticky, white tentacles are touched, they slowly retract.

While sea anemones (also in the *Class Anthozoa* with the corals) appear essentially the same at night as during the day, use your dive light to examine them closely at night, and you're likely to see the small symbiotic shrimp among their tentacles. On rare occasion, you might find larger symbiotic crabs as well.

Gastropods (*Phylum Mollusca*) such as nudibranchs are a mixed bag. Some are diurnal, and others like the Spanish dancer are strictly nocturnal. Most bivalves on the reef are attached to the substrate. These filter feeders appear equally inactive day and night, and most are encrusted with sponges, hydroids or something else making them difficult to see.

For the most part, cephalopods are nocturnal. Chambered nautiluses live in IndoPacific waters at depths of 500–1,500 feet during the day and migrate upward to about 200' below the surface at night—still too deep for a sport diver to observe. Dive operators will bait and trap them at night and bring them to the surface for clients to see. Cuttlefish are rarely seen at night, but squids, which travel mostly in schools and are often mistaken for fish, can be seen at dusk and early on night dives. Giant squid

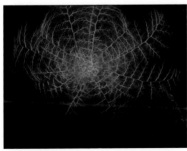 

FIGURE 2-11 *(S.M. Barnett)*
A basket star opens like a satellite dish to feed at night.

FIGURE 2-12 *(S.M. Barnett)*
A parrotfish asleep on the reef.

are nocturnal and remain in deep waters during the day. Only a few divers have managed to see and photograph them as they come to shallower waters at night.

The most intelligent invertebrates in the ocean, and in the world for that matter, are octopuses. While they are occasionally seen on daytime dives, these nocturnal predators are more frequently seen at night when they come out to hunt for fish, mollusks and crustaceans. Octopuses are much more rare in the IndoPacific because natives capture them for food.

Octopuses are undoubtedly one of the most delightful animals on the reef to interact with if a diver hasn't previously intimidated them. Both curious and easily frightened, they must be approached very slowly and deliberately. Make slow, deliberate movements, and present a bare hand, and you may get the octopus to approach you. Just be careful not to blind them with a light. If the octopus backs away, pull your hand back and wait. If you can get your bare hand within about 6 inches of the octopus and hold it still for a few minutes, the octopus may make contact with you. Its approach will be cautious, placing first one, then two, and three tentacles on your hand. Their suction cup touch will feel weird at first, but resist the temptation of pulling the octopus toward you, and it will likely pull itself up and onto the hand. You may see it change colors as it crawls all over, and it can gently be passed from one person to another. Since so many octopuses have been abused at the hands of humans—and they are smart—it's getting harder and harder to find octopuses that will interact freely like this. Octopuses have natural enemies as well, and are the favorite food of moray eels. Watch closely, and you'll see that morays are especially active at night.

Starfish, and their relatives in the *Phylum Echino-dermata*, tend to hide in the reef during the day and slowly come out at night to feed. Using modified spines around their mouth, they pick up small worms and organic material and put it in their complex stomachs. Some of them, like the Crown-of-Thorns, can turn their stomachs inside out through their mouths and digest living tissue outside their bodies. They can actually consume the living surface tissues of corals and the soft tissues of bivalves while they're still in their own shells! The bivalves must be opened slightly first, but their best efforts at resistance are no match for the starfish's strong arms with hundreds of tube feet.

Brittle stars and serpent stars hide in sponges and in the reef during the day and come out to feed on soft invertebrates at night. These small, modified sea stars, with central disks no larger than one inch in diameter, have five unbranching arms that tend to move in a single plane (i.e., two dimensions).

The most interesting members of this group are the much larger basket stars who have central discs up to 4.5 inches in diameter. Their arms, which stretch out up to 18 inches (0.5 meters), are highly branched, and can easily move in three dimensions. During the day, they roll up in a tight ball on a gorgonian or crawl into the reef. At night they actively crawl to some high vantage point either on a gorgonian or another part of the reef and open up like a satellite dish facing the tidal currents to filter the water for food. The large IndoPacific basket stars tend not to come out until 9–10 p.m. Shining a strong light through them and into the current is an exciting adventure if there is a lot of plankton in the water. These plankton will swim toward the light and the basket star will come alive as it tries to capture all these planktonic organisms drifting past its highly mobile branching arms. While the IndoPacific basket stars may reach over 3-1/2 feet in diameter, the Caribbean variety rarely exceed two feet.

Feather stars are the only crinoids seen on the reefs. Other crinoids, such as the stalked sea lilies, are only found in deep benthic (bottom) waters. The feather-like unbranching, flexible arms of the feather stars are used to filter the plankton—mostly copepods—from the water. During the day they are found lower down on the gorgonians with their arms retracted. Even in this inactive position, they can filter copepods from the passing currents. At night, the IndoPacific variety put on a real show. With slightly negative buoyancy, they either crawl slowly with their finger-like lower cimi (feet), or slowly move their arms to swim to the top of a gorgonian for a better position. Then they open up like umbrellas in the breeze to filter food drifting in the tidal current.

Diving into Darkness

The feather stars in the Caribbean are much less dramatic. They are smaller, less diverse and their central discs never leave the protection of the reef. Their arms stick out of the reef and filter the water day and night.

Sea urchins are the only herbivores among the echinoderms, but they play a major role in reef erosion, using their spines to drill out protective areas in the reef where they can hide during the daylight hours. When darkness comes, they head out onto the reef on suction-cupped feet to feed on algae. While the urchin's spines are very delicate, they can withstand a significant force if contacted straight on, easily penetrating a diver's exposure suit. When such a puncture occurs, chemicals in the thin living tissue that covers their primary calcium carbonate spine may result in irritation (see Appendix A for information on treating marine stings and punctures).

Sea cucumbers either hide in the reefs during the day or remain relatively inactive on the sand and rubble fields. At night, they use the modified tube feet surrounding their mouth to vacuum up the sand and debris off the bottom, digesting the organic material and passing the inorganic rubble through their digestive system. They protect themselves via the noxious chemicals in their skins. These skins, when properly cooked and prepared, produce a pronounced toxic and narcotic effect when eaten, and are thus in high demand in Asian markets. Sea cucumber (known as *beche-de-mer)* is highly regarded for its medicinal properties and is claimed to have anti-inflamitory properties.

An oddity of the sea cucumber is its manner of breathing (gas exchange), and this is particularly obvious at night. The sea cucumber has two respiratory trees for gaseous exchange which connect to the cloaca just before the cloacal (anal) opening. The sea cucumbers literally suck fresh seawater in their cloaca to fill their respiratory trees. Then they blow it back out the same opening. A curious sight generally seen only at night is a sea cucumber breathing with the posterior half of the body sticking up off the reef and the anterior part holding onto the reef.

Also of note is the relationship between pearlfish and sea cucumbers. The pearlfish backs itself tail-first through the cloaca into the respiratory trees of certain sea cucumbers. The nature of the relationship between these two species is unclear. While the sea cucumber provides protection for the pearlfish, there is no known benefit to the sea cucumber, leading experts to believe that the relationship is a form of commensalism.

Some of the benthic rays tend to be active feeders at night, especially the yellow ray of the Caribbean. They are often observed cruising over the sand flats looking for food. The Atlantic/Southern ray of Stingray City fame seems to be diurnal. The large pelagic eagle and manta rays must swim to "breathe," so they don't settle down on the bottom. Eagle rays are rare at night, but mantas can be attracted with bright lights to dive boats at night. Although mantas tend to feed mostly during the day, the strong lights attract concentrations of plankton that entice the mantas.

Major shifts occur in the populations of fish seen on a reef at night. Large groups of schooling fishes of almost any kind are rarely seen at night. In fact, many of the fish commonly seen on daytime dives become inactive at night, and may be seen sleeping or in a trance-like state, and may appear to have different color patterns than seen during the day. Triggerfishes like to bed down in small crevices at night, and raise their spines to lock them safely into position. Angelfishes, butterfly fishes, surgeon fishes, Seabasses, groupers, parrotfishes, blennies, gobies, trumpetfishes, snappers, grunts, seahorses (hardly active day or night), and hawkfishes are rarely active at night. They may be found lying on their sides or wedged between parts of the reef with eyes wide open (they have no eyelids). If disturbed and blinded by dive lights, they may shoot out from the reef and slam into the diver.

Of particular note is the parrotfish, which is occasionally seen at night sleeping in the transparent mucous cocoon it secrets. Why the cocoons are seen so infrequently is not precisely known, and there's no strong evidence of their exact purpose. However, some believe the cocoon contains the parrotfishes scent, which makes it harder for predators to detect.

Diving into Darkness

Another nighttime notable is the flashlight fish (*Anomalops katoptron* and *Photoblepharon palpebratus*), found in crevices of coral reefs and other low light areas. These small fish have cheek pouches filled with bacteria that emit an intense blue-green light. You may see the lights blink as the fish raise and lower lids that cover the pouches, or as they roll the light source in the socket. The bioluminescent light attracts food, identifies mates, and inadvertently draws the attention of predators (and divers!).

Fish that tend to be active at night include tarpons, squirrelfishes, soldierfishes, scorpionfishes, frogfishes, lizardfishes, crocodilefishes, puffers, goatfishes, flounders, hogfishes, and filefishes. These nocturnal fish may also change colors at night.

While sharks may be a common sight while diving on a reef during the day, they are infrequently seen on night dives. One explanation might be that they are out there and out of range of the lights we use while diving. In a non-feeding situation, sharks are likely to keep their distance and are generally non-threatening.

One species of shark may be of particular concern to night divers. The Tiger shark, found in various habitats in tropical and subtropical waters, is considered one of the most dangerous species of shark. Especially at home along vertical walls and drop-offs by day, the Tiger shark ascends the walls to feed at night. Some speculate that sightings of Tiger sharks are becoming more common because overfishing has depleted their deep-water food sources. As Dr. George Burgess of the International Shark Files at the University of Florida, Gainesville, FL notes, divers should consider alternative night dive sites to walls where Tiger sharks are known to frequent.

Numerous marine species have learned to take advantage of shore lighting to illuminate nocturnal hunting grounds. The waters adjacent to a particular restaurant on the Kona coast of Hawaii are frequented by mantas that forage in the glow of the lights. In some areas, the interaction of divers has caused a fascinating adaptation by local species. Dee Scarr describes her experience on the reefs of Bonaire, where jacks have learned to follow divers at night and hunt in the beams of their dive lights. The glow of eyes of shrimp and other creatures illuminated by lights would make easy targets for the jacks, who would dart into the beam of light to snatch their prey.

Scarr also writes of the antics of "Charlie," a local tarpon, who stayed glued to her side during night dives to hunt grunts in the beam of her light. Apparently, other fish were of little interest, but Charlie quickly devoured the delectable grunts. After a while, other tarpon learned Charlie's trick and would tag along on dives. Scarr altered her diving technique to save the grunts from the tarpon, but the experience provided an object lesson in the types of fish on which a tarpon would prey.

Likewise, on the outer reefs of Belize, a dive light is referred to as a "ray gun," because of the many tarpon that follow night divers and consume the small fish illuminated by the lights.

Similarly, Scarr found that eel catfish and lionfish in the IndoPacific quickly learned to follow night divers and would hunt various baitfish and planktonic creatures by the beams of their lights.

Depending on the location and the time of the dive, the activities seen and experienced will be much different. For example, numerous species of fish spawn only at dusk, before many of the filter-feeding species begin their nocturnal feeding, thus giving their eggs the best possible advantage for survival. This is also a good time to see various predators, such as barracuda, jacks, groupers, and dolphins, actively hunting their respective prey. By starting a night dive before darkness has actually settled in, divers can get a rare view of the underwater world.

Many changes don't take place until later at night, perhaps two to three hours after sunset. This is the best time to look for parrotfish sleeping in their mucus cocoons, to observe the large IndoPacific basket stars, and to see some of the more dramatic flowering of some coral species. A still different perspective can be obtained by making a pre-dawn night dive. As author Linda Litteral Lambert notes, some species, like the snappers, feed primarily in the pre-dawn hours, breaking from their protective schools to hunt in solitary fashion. Other species, such as basket stars, can be seen slinking off to their daytime dens as then make the transition from nocturnal feeding to daytime hiding.

CHAPTER 3

Night Diving Equipment

3.0 Introduction

When we think of the equipment needed for a night dive, we generally think of dive lights. Dive lights are an essential ingredient, but additional equipment may also greatly increase our comfort and safety on a night dive. And while we typically use the same equipment at night as on a daytime dive, some minor modifications to our gear can make it much better suited to the night diving environ-

FIGURE 3-1 *(J. Hewlett)*
Night diving requires an array of specialized equipment, including lights, not normally required for a daytime dive.

ment. In this chapter we'll focus on selecting the right equipment and making the needed modifications for safe, enjoyable night diving.

3.1 Dive Lights

3.1.1. Classification of Dive Lights
The most obvious piece of equipment for a night dive is an underwater light. While nothing seems quite as simple as a "flashlight" designed for underwater use, there's much more to a reliable dive light than you might expect, and there are many options from which to choose.

Dive lights are typically classified as to their general purpose: primary lights, backup or day lights, and specialty lights. Primary lights are generally larger and more powerful, providing the primary illumination for night diving activities. Backup or day-lights are generally smaller and less powerful than primary lights. These are often used by divers on daytime dives to peer into cracks and crevices.

Specialty dive lights are generally small lights of various configurations, and serve a multitude of purposes. These in clude identification lights, instrument or gauge lights, navigation or marker lights, personal marker/emergency lights, and ultra-violet lights for viewing fluorescence in marine organisms.

3.1.2 Basic Light Components
Before we launch into the process of choosing a dive light, it's important to understand the basic components and technology involved in light design.

A basic dive light has five primary elements: a lamp, reflector/lens assembly, power source, switch and waterproof case. The lamp, or bulb, converts electrical energy to light energy. The reflector/lens focuses and directs this light energy. The power source provides the electrical power for the lamp, and the switch completes the electrical circuit that provides the power to the lamp. The entire assembly is enclosed in a waterproof case designed to withstand the pressure and rigors of underwater use. If that sounds too simple, rest assured there's actually quite a bit more involved.

FIGURE 3-2
A basic dive light has five primary elements: a lamp, reflector/lens assembly, power source, switch, and waterproof case.

(R.N. Rossier)

3.1.2.1 Lamp Design and Technology

While there are many variations in lamp design, most operate on the same basic principle. A basic lamp consists of a fine tungsten coil filament inside the vacuum of an evacuated glass container. When electrical current is passed through the filament, it heats up and glows, emitting light energy in the infrared, visible, and ultraviolet spectrums. A major focus in lamp technology has been to maximize the efficiency, or the amount of visible light produced per watt-hour of power. This has meant shifting the frequency of the emitted energy out of the infrared spectrum into the visible spectrum. One way to accomplish this is to raise the temperature of the filament by passing more current though it, but this alone has limitations.

As a tungsten filament burns, the tungsten vaporizes and is deposited on the interior of the glass bulb, resulting in a dark residue that reduces light output. One way to reduce tungsten vaporization is to introduce an inert gas, such as argon, into the bulb. Since argon is an insulator, it allows the filament to glow hotter, while reducing the tungsten deposits on the glass. The bottom line is more light for fewer watts.

While the use of argon significantly improves the efficiency of lamps, other inert gasses such as krypton and xenon perform better still. Although more expensive, a xenon filled lamp burns hotter and whiter than an argon or krypton bulb. But high wattage xenon lamps still suffer to a small degree from tungsten deposits.

The next generation in lamp design introduced halogen gas into the bulb. The halogen causes the evaporating tungsten to redeposit on the filament. Since the halogen attacks the glass, a more expensive glass with iodine or bromine is needed, and this adds to the cost of the lamp. High-energy lamps, such as those used for automobile headlights, require quartz glass to withstand the high temperatures.

One approach to improving lamp design is to eliminate the tungsten filament entirely. One example, fluorescent lighting, has been used for camping and other outdoor applications, and a few fluorescent dive lights have been developed. The advantage of fluorescent lighting is incredible efficiency. Tungsten produces around 18 to 20 lumens (a measure of light energy) per watt, whereas fluorescent lights produce around 100 to 150 lumens per watt. The down side of the fluorescent lights is their poor spectral quality, which can result less desirable illumination characteristics and unnatural color appearance.

Another lighting technology, called HID for high intensity discharge, uses no filament at all. Instead, a lamp filled with a small amount of mercury and rare earth chlorides contains two electrodes. An electronic circuit generates an electrical arc that jumps the gap between the electrodes, thus causing the illumination. The composition of the gases in the lamp can be changed to produce the desired spectral characteristics, but generally deliver a color temperature of 6,500K (compared to

FIGURE 3-3
One of the latest developments in high reliability, high output lighting systems is the High Intensity Discharge (HID) light.

(Dive Rite)

3,000K for a quartz halogen lamp). HID lights have two major advantages over tungsten filament lights. First, the light output is significantly higher, in the order of 60 to 80 lumens per watt. Second, HID lamps are highly reliable since they have no filament to break. One precaution when using an HID light is to closely monitor the rated burn time of the power source (battery). An HID lamp will continue to burn brightly even as the battery power is depleted. The result can be an unwitting discharge of the battery below the recommended minimum voltage.

The major down side is the dollars. HID dive lights are considerably more expensive than other types of lighting technology, but they are favored by technical divers and others who demand high reliability, high efficiency and high light output.

One of the latest developments in dive light technology is the white LED (Light Emitting Diode). As with the HID, the lamp has no filament and is therefore incredibly reliable and able to easily withstand shock and vibration that would destroy a conventional light. The white LED is also very efficient. A two "AA" cell white LED light that puts out the same illumination as a

FIGURE 3-4 *(R.N. Rossier)*
This white LED dive light uses a 7-LED array.

conventional incandescent light will typically run more than ten times as long (30 hours or more), giving off a bright, blue-white beam (6200k color temperature) that's easy on the eyes. Unlike the HID, the white LED doesn't require an expensive electronic circuit to drive it. White LED lights, while more expensive than incandescent dive lights, are still reasonably priced. They come in a variety of sizes, but as of this writing, a high intensity broad beam white LED light is not available. If reliability and long burn time are primary considerations, the white LED light is an excellent choice, but if you need lots of lumens, you may require an HID or incandescent light.

3.1.2.2 Reflector and Lens

The purpose of the reflector and lens is to focus or direct the light in the desired beam width. The shape of the reflector and lens determines the beam width, as well as the "softness" of the light. A highly polished reflector with a clear lens will provide a bright beam, often with a dark spot in the center caused by the shadow of the filament. A textured reflector or lens results in a softer, diffused light beam void of shadows. Some lights are designed with a lens-focusing feature, which allows the diver to vary the beam width to suit the needs of the moment.

3.1.2.3 Battery Design and Technology

A key element in any dive light has always been a reliable power supply. For years, the industry standard was replaceable batteries, and the carbon-zinc dry cell was the name of the game. These are relatively inexpensive batteries, but simply don't have the energy needed for modern dive lights to provide adequate burn time. Newer alkaline batteries were developed to meet the demands of modern "high drain" applications including games, toys, electronics and flashlights.

In years past, a mercury coating over the zinc was used to prevent gaseous hydrogen formation during the chemical process that generates electricity. Environmental concerns forced manufacturers to use alternative technologies to prevent hydrogen generation. These innovations worked, but not quite as well as mercury, and the consequence was that the newer batteries had a greater tendency to fail by giving off hydrogen gas. The batteries all have a safety vent designed to release hydrogen if the pressure builds too high. This is moot point in normal applications, but in the sealed environment of a dive light, the hydrogen gas creates a potential hazard. If the hydrogen escapes into the sealed, waterproof case, it can react explosively with oxygen. Many dive light manufacturers tackled the problem by installing a catalyst (palladium on aluminum) which slowly combines hydrogen at low concentrations with oxygen. This prevents the hydrogen from reaching explosive concentrations. However, when a battery fails—such as when a light floods with sea water—hydrogen can be produced rapidly enough to overwhelm the catalyst, resulting in a potentially dangerous situation (see flooded light first aid).

There have been instances where batteries have failed spontaneously, probably due to a failure of the coating on the zinc. Fortunately, most of these problems are behind us now, and newer batteries are highly reliable. Divers should still exercise caution when installing batteries in dive lights. Installing a battery backwards often results in a battery failure, this again may rapidly produce copious quantities of hydrogen.

Diving into Darkness

When purchasing replaceable batteries for a dive light, make sure you're getting what you think you're getting. Alkaline and carbon-zinc flashlight batteries look nearly identical, but their performance is worlds apart. The alkaline battery, which costs more, packs 2 to 3 times the energy of a carbon-zinc battery, depending on the size of the cell and its use. The alkaline battery should say "alkaline" on it, whereas the carbon-zinc varieties bear such names as Heavy Duty, Super Heavy Duty, and Classic.

Rechargeable batteries are also used extensively in dive lights. For years, the standard of the industry was the lead-acid gel cell, which uses a gelatinous electrolyte rather than liquid sulfuric acid. Lead-acid gel cells are still used in many underwater lighting applications, especially in technical and wreck diving. Many rechargeable recreational dive lights now use nickel-cadmium (nicad) batteries, which offer several advantages. Nicads can be recharged up to 1,000 times if well cared for, they have a high power capacity, and they can be discharged at a high rate.

FIGURE 3-5   *(R.N. Rossier)*
Choosing the optimum battery for a dive light application can be challenging.

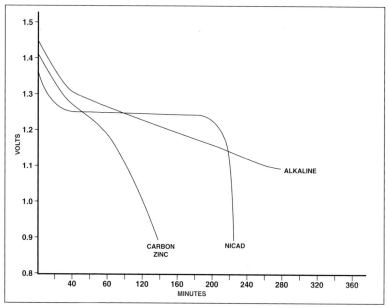

FIGURE 3-6
Typical discharge characteristics comparing carbon zinc, nicad, and alkaline batteries. (Discharge characteristics vary markedly and are affected by numerous factors including cell size, lamp type, temperature, and continuity of use.)

A major difference between nicads and replaceable alkaline batteries is the rate at which they deliver energy (see FIGURE 3-6). A nicad has a "flat" discharge curve, meaning it maintains voltage and will deliver energy quickly over a greater percentage of its useful charge. This means a brighter light that stays brighter longer. On the flip side, the nicads' voltage drops off rapidly towards the end of their useful charge, causing them to dim very quickly. Lead-acid gel cells and alkaline batteries have a more sloped discharge curve. They don't provide energy as quickly as a nicad, and the voltage drops gradually over the discharge cycle. A light powered by a gel cell or alkaline batteries will begin to burn yellow sooner, and will dim slowly over a longer period of time, thus providing the diver ample warning of an impending failure.

A problem with early nicad batteries was that charge-discharge patterns created a "memory" which can decrease the capacity of the battery. While there is still some degree of memory associated with nicad batteries, this characteristic is much less pronounced in modern designs. What's important is what happens in the first few charges. The first few times a light with a nicad battery is used, it should be discharged until the bulb burns yellow, then given a full recharge. This will ensure that the battery charges to full capacity.

Rechargeable alkalines are also readily available today, and these batteries represent a compromise between alkaline and rechargeable nicads. The storage degradation of these batteries in a high-drain service such as a dive light will probably not allow you to get full capacity and value for the higher cost.

Nickel-metal hydride batteries represent the state of the art for many topside applications including cellular phones, computers, camcorders and other high-drain electronics applications. These batteries use a metal hydride rather than cadmium to get twice the storage capacity of modern-day nicad. The down side includes higher cost (roughly three times that of a nicad) and problems in charging. If the charging isn't carefully controlled, hydrogen will be rapidly released from the battery, creating a serious explosion risk. An expensive charger is required to control the charging, and even with that, the off-gassing of hydrogen makes these batteries unsuitable for any underwater applications such as dive lights and underwater video cameras.

3.1.2.4 Switch and Waterproof Case

The components of a dive light must be housed in some form of a waterproof case. All dive lights rely on an O-ring seal to maintain the integrity of the light, but there are differences in design.

One popular design approach is to integrate the switch with the end cap that houses the lamp, reflector and lens. These lights often incorporate multiple O-rings, and are a simple and reliable design. Another highly reliable switch is a magnetic

FIGURE 3-7   *(R.N. Rossier)*
A double O-ring seal adds reliability to the integrated switch/endcap assembly.

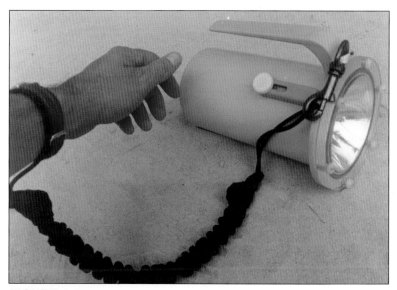

FIGURE 3-8   *(R.N. Rossier)*
This light is activated by a locking magnetic reed switch. A brass clip attached to the light allows it to be clipped to a D-ring when not in use.

FIGURE 3-9   *(R.N. Rossier)*
A lanyard guards against accidental loss of a dive light.

reed switch. The moveable contacts are located within the waterproof housing, and are operated via a sliding magnet assembly on the exterior of the case.

Regardless of the design, look for a reliable switch. A switch that incorporates a lock to prevent inadvertent activation can be an important feature. It's always frustrating to arrive at the dive site only to find the batteries in you dive light dead because the switch was inadvertently turned on.

Another important feature is a lanyard or strap with clip. Many divers like a wrist lanyard, which prevents them from loosing the light if they drop it accidentally or in an emergency. A strap and clip allows you to secure the light to a D-ring.

3.1.3 Specialty Lights
In addition to the primary and secondary dive light, night divers may use an assortment of specialty lights. These lights serve a multitude of purposes from illuminating gauges and camera controls, to identifying divers and down lines. Specialty lights are low power lights, typically 10 watts or less, and may be white, colored, steady or flashing.

Night Diving Equipment

One form of specialty light is the single-use chemical light stick. These generally consist of a liquid-filled plastic tube within which is contained a smaller breakable vial of activating chemical. When the tube is bent sufficiently, the inner vial breaks, releasing the activating chemical to produce a low temperature glow similar to a firefly or bioluminescent algae. Depending on the particular light stick, the glow may last from four to eight hours or more. Chemical light sticks are great for illuminating gauges, and are often attached to regulator yoke to act as a personal identification light.

Chemical light sticks come in a variety of colors and sizes. When diving in a class, with a guide, or in a group, the instructors or leaders are typically equipped with a different color light

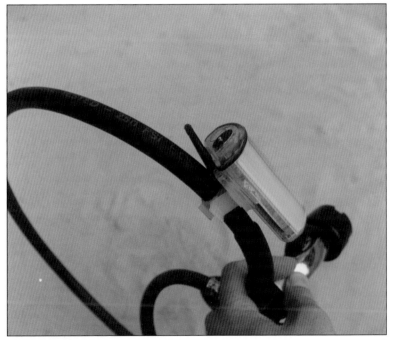

FIGURE 3-10   *(R.N. Rossier)*
This water-activated personal marker light clips onto a regulator hose.

stick from the rest of the group, providing ready identification in times of need. When using chemical light sticks, be certain to remove them from the water and dispose of them properly. Improper use and disposal of chemical light sticks has resulted in them being banned in some popular resort locations such as Bonaire.

Manufacturers now produce a variety of low-power identification lights, which can be attached to a mask strap, snorkel, BC, hose, or other location for ready identification. Both steady and flashing lights, and models with colored lenses are available.

Marker strobes represent another form of specialty dive light. These are typically used to identify anchor lines, down lines, surface floats, or other locations, and can be a great aid to underwater or surface navigation. Personal strobes can be used to mark your location and signal for help in an emergency. These come in a variety of sizes, colors, and powers to meet virtually any underwater need. Keep in mind that a white flashing strobe on the surface is usually interpreted as a distress signal.

Perhaps one of the most interesting specialty lights is the ultraviolet or "black light" used to observe fluorescence in marine organisms. Not to be confused with bioluminescence,

(Pelican)   (Underwater Kinetics)   (Pelican)

FIGURE 3-11
Hand-held primary lights come in a variety of configurations.

FIGURE 3-12 *(J. Hewlett)*
A light with remote battery canister offers enhanced flexibility and ease of use.

fluorescence is the phenomenon that occurs when an object absorbs light at one wavelength and then re-emits light at another wavelength. Probably the most common example is a black light poster or the bright glowing of a white piece of clothing when lit by an ultraviolet light. Numerous marine organisms exhibit fluorescence, including corals, anemones, nudibranchs, shrimps, tunicates, and bristleworms, to name a few. For more information on marine fluorescence and underwater blacklights, visit the NightSea web site at www.nightsea.com.

3.1.4 Light Selection

Regardless of the type of dive light you're looking for—primary, secondary, or specialty—a number of factors must be considered. These include the basic configuration, power source, intensity (lumens or watts), beam width (focus), depth rating, handling characteristics and color.

Configuration—The configuration, particularly for a primary light, is largely a matter of personal preference, and the style of diving you plan. Probably the most popular primary dive light

 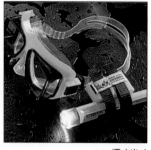 

(Pelican)   (Tektite)   (Niterider)

FIGURE 3-13
Head-mounted lights allow hands-free operation.

configuration is the hand-held self-contained light, but many technical divers prefer lights which have a remote battery secured to their tank, weight belt, or a harness. Divers who prefer to keep their hands free should consider the various head-mounted designs available on the market.

Modular lighting systems, such as the Dive Rite MLS, offer a variety of features and are also favored by many wreck, cave and technical divers. These lighting systems are comprised of battery canisters, light heads, and switches, which can be assembled in various configurations. Battery canisters mate to accommodate various quantities of batteries, and various head and switch combinations are mated to suit the needs of a particular dive.

Power Supply—A primary consideration in selecting any dive light is an adequate power source. It's always disappointing when a light dies out before you run low on air and bottom time. Check the burn time for the light, and make sure it has adequate power to meet the demands of your typical dive profile. For rechargeable lights, consider purchasing spare battery packs to allow swapping to a fresh power supply for repetitive dives.

When choosing between rechargeable or replaceable batteries, remember that rechargeable lights are initially more expensive, but don't incur the expense of battery replacement.

(PATCO, Inc.)   *(Dive Rite)*

FIGURE 3-14
Modular lights allow divers to choose from a selection of battery packs, lamps, and reflectors to assemble a light suitable for the specific needs of the dive.

If you plan to use the light frequently, the rechargeable design may be a more economical choice. Lights with replaceable batteries usually cost less initially, but the long term cost of replacement batteries can make them more expensive in the long run. If you won't be using your light frequently, the replaceable battery design may be a good choice.

For some divers, reliability and discharge characteristics are more important than cost. Many cave and technical divers prefer lights with replaceable alkaline batteries because of the more desirable discharge characteristics. Cave divers typically prefer to have their lights remain burning, even if the beam is dim and yellow, rather than to have the light shine brightly until it abruptly extinguishes. Despite the added cost, these divers often insist on fresh batteries for each dive for maximum reliability and burn time.

Diving into Darkness

Intensity and Beam Width—The intensity and focus of the light beam is another important factor. While many divers prefer a wide beam light in the 12 to 50 watt range or higher for night dives, others find a smaller light and narrow beam satisfactory, especially in clear water. A narrower beam light with 4 to 12 watts power is often selected for a backup or secondary light which can also be used for daytime dives to peek into cracks and crevices. Specialty lights often run in the 1 to 10 watt range, depending on the specific use.

If you're looking for a primary dive light that can also be used for daytime dives, consider a model with and adjustable lens. This feature allows you to select a wide beam for broad illumination, or a narrow beam for close inspection work.

If you dive frequently with the same buddy or buddies, choose lights with similar intensity, since stronger ones easily overshadow weaker lights. Look for a light that produces smooth, even illumination over the entire beam width. Remember that white lights provide better illumination and reveal true colors.

Depth Rating—Only lights designed as underwater lights should be trusted to provide reliable service underwater. For maximum durability and reliability, choose one rated to at least twice your normal diving depth.

Handling—The size, configuration, and buoyancy affect the handling characteristics of a dive light, and focus on such ergonomics considerations has been a growing trend in dive light design. For a hand-held light, make sure the grip or handle is comfortable, and that the switch can be operated easily, yet not inadvertently. Neutral buoyancy is perhaps the most comfortable, but a positively buoyant light will float to the surface if accidentally dropped. Some divers prefer a light with slightly negative buoyancy so they can rest it on the bottom while they tend to other tasks. A clip and/or wrist lanyard provides a convenient means to secure the light where it is easily accessible and can help avoid accidental loss.

Color—Color is a matter of personal preference, but black or other dark colored lights can be difficult to find if dropped. Bright colors like orange, yellow, and green can make a lost light easier to find.

3.1.5 Dive Light Care and Maintenance

3.1.5.1 General Care and Maintenance

A dive light is a relatively easy piece of equipment to maintain. Field maintenance generally involves only battery replacement/recharge, replacement of failed bulbs, cleaning of O-rings, and post-dive washing.

When it comes to ensuring reliable operation, divers must pay particular attention to the batteries and power packs. While replaceable alkaline batteries are very reliable, they must be installed properly. Installing a battery backwards can lead to a battery failure which may damage the inner workings of the light, and result in an explosive concentration of hydrogen in the case.

After battery failures, the most common cause of a light failure is a broken or burned out filament. Filaments break primarily due to excessive voltage, excessive heat, or vibration. Some dive lights can only be used when submerged in water due to the tremendous heat generated. Consult the manufacturer's instructions regarding this precaution. Since bulbs carried as spares are often subject to a great deal of impacts and vibration, some divers carry less expensive argon-filled bulbs as spares. Although these will work in a pinch, to ensure a light will provide its rated illumination you must replace the burned-out bulb with the proper type (argon, xenon, halogen, etc., and proper voltage). After installing the new bulb, clean it thoroughly to remove any oil, grease or fingerprints that could cause the bulb to overheat and fail prematurely. Also, when replacing the bulbs or performing other maintenance, be careful no to touch the reflector. Oil from fingerprints can damage the reflector and reduce its effectiveness.

The integrity of your light relies primarily on proper maintenance of the O-ring(s) which forms the watertight seal.

Diving into Darkness

These should be periodically cleaned with a clean, soft, lint-free cloth and inspected for nicks, cuts, deformities or cracks. Lightly lubricate the O-ring with clear silicone grease, and clean the mating surface with the corner of a clean, soft cloth. Excess silicone grease on the O-ring does nothing to improve the seal, and serves only to attract sand and grit that will cause the O-ring to wear more quickly. Avoid using lubricants other than silicone grease as some lubricants can chemically damage the O-rings as well as many of the plastics used in dive lights.

Battery Use and Care Tips

- Always follow the manufacturer's instructions and be sure to install the batteries correctly.
- Never attempt to recharge a battery unless it is specifically marked "rechargeable." Doing so can result in rupture or leakage of the battery. Always use the proper recharger. Never use a nicad battery charger to charge an alkaline rechargeable.
- Keep battery contacts clean by gently rubbing them with a soft cloth or clean rubber eraser.
- Replace batteries with the correct size and type. Replace all the batteries at once. Never mix old and new or various types (alkaline, rechargeable alkaline, carbon zinc, etc.). Mixing old or new batteries or batteries of different types could cause rupture or leakage that damages the light.
- Batteries should be stored in a dry place at normal room temperature. Always keep batteries away from hot places.
- Remove batteries for transport or for extended storage periods.
- Handle batteries with care. Never carry loose batteries in a pocket or gear bag containing loose change or other metallic objects. Doing so could cause the batteries to short-circuit, and excessive heat or a fire could result.
- Never dispose of batteries in fire. They may rupture or leak.

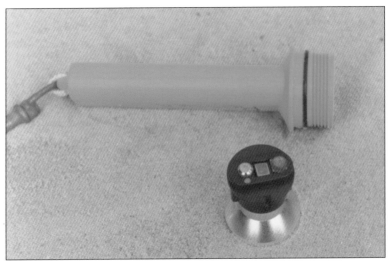

FIGURE 3-15   *(R.N. Rossier)*
Corroded contacts are a common cause of light problems.

Electrical connections, including the switch mechanism/con-
tacts and bulb contacts may also require occasional attention to
remove any oil, grease or corrosion byproducts. Contacts can
be cleaned with electrical contact cleaner, or lightly buffed with
emery cloth, fine sandpaper, steel wool, a rough cloth, or rubber
eraser. Residue from this process should be removed before
reassembly.

After a dive, clean your light with fresh water and dry it off
thoroughly before packing it for storage or transport. When not
in use, or when traveling, it's best to remove the batteries from
the light to prevent inadvertent operation, and to avoid damage
in the event that a battery fails and leaks acid.

It's best to pack and transport your light with the batteries (or
at least one battery) removed. If you do travel with the batteries
installed in your light, loosen the lens assembly until the light
turns off, then be sure the switch is in the off (and locked, if possible) position. A piece of tape over the switch will also help
prevent inadvertent activation during transport.

FIGURE 3-16 *(R.N. Rossier)*
Dirty or corroded contacts can be cleaned with a rubber eraser, emery cloth, fine sandpaper, or steel wool.

3.1.5.2 Flooded Light First Aid

On rare occasion, a light will leak and become flooded. The most common causes for flooding include a failed O-ring seal or improper closure of the watertight case. First aid for such an occurrence begins with immediately turning the light off and switching to a backup light.

Once safely on the surface, drain the light, remove the batteries, disassemble as practical, and rinse the light and internal components with fresh water. Rechargeable batteries can be rinsed with isopropyl alcohol to promote drying. The casing and components can be air dried, or use a hair dryer on low heat. Be sure to determine the cause of the flooding and make appropriate repairs before returning the light to service. If the problem cannot be readily determined or repaired, return the light to a professional dive center or manufacturer for service or replacement.

3.2 Night Diving Support Equipment

3.2.1 Lights
A night dive requires a variety of support equipment in addition to the basic night diving lights. Some type of broad beam floodlights are needed in the staging area where divers will be gearing up. These can be battery-powered incandescent lights, fluorescent lights, or even propane or white gas powered lights. In addition to providing the necessary illumination for gearing up and repacking equipment at the end of the dive, the floodlights perform a critical function in the event that a diver requires some form of medical attention. Many divers find that a standard flashlight can also be useful when gearing up and performing predive equipment checks. Using a flashlight instead of a dive light helps conserve battery power for the dive.

In some environments, signal lights used by a tender to signal divers in the water may also be appropriate. Navigation or range lights are used to provide directional guidance to divers who must navigate on the surface along a particular bearing to avoid obstacles.

3.2.2 Ascent/Descent Lines
The most difficult parts of a night dive can be the descent and ascent. Unless the diver has some form of fixed reference, such as the bottom or a fixed line, it can be difficult to maintain orientation and descent/ascent rate, and disorientation or vertigo can result. For this reason, a fixed down line is often secured to a boat or float. When diving from a boat, the anchor line is sometimes used for this purpose. Often times, marker lights or strobes are attached at the bottom or some intermediate position along this line to aid divers in returning to the line at the end of the dive.

3.2.3 Emergency Ascent Equipment
Even when conducting a shore dive, or diving with a down line, a situation can arise wherein a diver must make an immediate ascent, or is unable to find the anchor line or down line from the boat or surface float. For this reason, divers are encouraged to carry some form or emergency ascent gear.

A small lift bag and line reel clipped to a D-ring at the base of the cylinder (or other convenient location) can readily serve as a reference for just such an emergency ascent. The diver can introduce a small amount of air into the lift bag, release the line as the bag goes to the surface, then ascend using the line as a reference.

If the lift bag is equipped with a strobe or reflective material, it can also be used as an emergency signal in the event that a diver becomes entangled at the bottom and separated from his buddy.

Also consider adding a longer hose (7 to 9 feet) to your alternate air regulator. A longer hose will make it easier to swim independently and control buoyancy during an emergency ascent. The excess length of hose can be readily secured to the bottom of your cylinder using a length of surgical tubing (see FIGURE 3-17).

3.2.4 First Aid/Emergency Communication
Beyond the normal first aid and emergency communication equipment carried for a daytime dive, special equipment is needed to meet the demands of a problem at night. For the diver, emergency signaling equipment including waterproof signal flares, a safety sausage, and whistle or Dive Alert[TM] can be used to signal personnel on the boat or shore in the event of an emergency.

Flood lights should be included as part of the surface-based emergency equipment to assist in providing medical attention to an injured or distressed diver. Signal flares and other forms of night emergency communication equipment should also be part of the standard equipment carried on a dive boat at night.

3.3 General Equipment Preparation
Although we use the same primary equipment for a night dive as we do during the day, a number of simple and inexpensive modifications are necessary to accommodate a night dive. In addition, we can also make some minor alterations to our gear that simplifies night diving.

3.3.1 Identification

In the dim lighting of the pre- or post-dive environment, dive gear can easily be misidentified, lost, or inadvertently picked up by another diver. For this reason, it's important to make certain that all your gear is clearly labeled. Take a few minutes during your initial equipment check at home to mark your gear with an indelible marker or other reliable means.

Other modifications can make it easier to identify you both underwater and on the surface. Remember that proper identification is essential to maintaining the proper buddy contact through the dive. Reflective strips added to your BC, fins, cylinder, exposure suit, or other items can greatly enhance underwater identification at night, and can help prevent

FIGURE 3-17
A line reel, small lift bag, and extended hose on the alternate air regulator will help a diver make a controlled ascent during a night diving emergency.

(J. Hewlett)

accidental loss of your equipment. Likewise, a personal identification light attached to your BC, cylinder, or regulator yoke will aid in locating and identifying you. An identification light on your surface float or dive flag will make it easier for boaters and friends on the surface to keep track of your position and movement during the dive.

Other accessory lights can also be important. Even if your pressure gauge, instrument console, or computer has a luminous display, an instrumentation light can make it easier to read.

3.3.2 Equipment Rigging Tips
Not only is it important to have the right lights for a night dive, it's critically important to have them properly secured. Most divers like to have a wrist lanyard on their primary light, but a clip can also be useful. If the light fails, you may want to clip it out of the way until the dive is over.

Backup lights can also be secured with a clip, or a combination of clips and straps made of rubber surgical tubing or other suitable materials. Backup lights should be in a location where you can readily retrieve them in total darkness with one hand.

Since you may be carrying more gear than you normally do on a daytime dive, the addition of clips and D-rings can provide a simple means of attaching the gear in a secure yet easily accessible manner. D-rings attached to the BC, or to a band near the base of your cylinder, provide a convenient location to secure dive lights, line reels, lift bags, and other accessory equipment to which are attached the appropriate clips.

Other items of your basic dive gear can also be modified to enhance safety on a night dive. A glow-in-the-dark mouthpiece guard or retainer for your alternate air source can make it easier to find in an emergency. Also consider securing your dive computer or instrument console. Dangling gauges are a problem on any dive, but the last thing we need is to get snagged on a night dive. Remember that if you're holding onto a dive light,

FIGURE 3-18
A clip, D-ring, and short loop of surgical tubing provide a convenient method for securing a back-up light to a BC's cummerbund.

(R.N. Rossier)

you're already short-handed. By clipping your computer or console in an orientation that allows you to see it without holding onto it, you ease the burden on your one free hand.

Give the placement of your knife some thought for night diving as well. Having your knife readily accessible in a location where you can find it with your eyes shut is a good practice. Remember, too, that you can't always spot entanglement hazards as easily at night, and may be more likely to become tangled up and need that knife to extricate yourself.

FIGURE 3-19   *(R.N. Rossier)*
A brightly colored alternate air regulator can be easier to locate in poor lighting conditions.

3.3.3 Spare Equipment

In addition to the spare equipment you normally carry on a dive, bring along the parts needed to repair and maintain your dive lights. A couple sets of fresh batteries, spare bulbs, and O-rings will go a long way toward keeping your lights in operation. If you use rechargeable batteries, a spare set may still be useful so you can use one set while the other is recharging.

Also carry the tools and supplies needed to perform the basic field maintenance of your lights. If you're using rechargeable batteries, be sure to bring along a charger and spare set of batteries. You'll also want clear silicone grease for the O-rings, soft cloths for cleaning components, and emery cloth, fine sandpaper, steel wool, a rough cloth, or rubber eraser to clean dirty or corroded contacts. Avoid the use of cotton swabs, which can leave fibers on O-rings and mating surfaces resulting in leaks. Instead, use a soft lint free cloth or lens tissue. Spare O-rings and lamps (bulbs) for each type of light you carry can be indispensable. Finally, bring along a spare light, just in case one fails and cannot be repaired in time for a planned dive.

NOTES

CHAPTER 4

Human Factors and the Night Diver

4.0 Introduction

At first blush, night diving might not seem like such a big deal. It's dark, so we use dive lights. No problem, right? But nothing is that simple in diving. In reality, some very important differences distinguish day from night diving. Diving at night introduces an entirely new regime of human factors considerations that affect our physiological, psychological and biomechanical adaptation to the underwater environment. By understanding these human factors considerations, we can improve our aquatic decision-making and safety in the water after dark.

4.1 The Rhythm of the Night

One of the first implications in night diving is the effect of our circadian rhythms—our

FIGURE 4-1 *(J. Hewlett)*
Equipment considerations and task loading are two important human factors considerations in night diving.

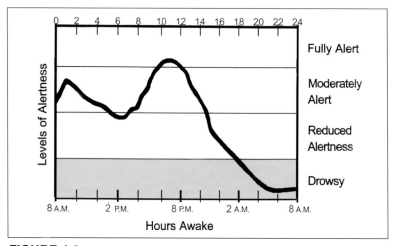

FIGURE 4-2
Mental alertness decreases rapidly as a dive continues later into the night. (Reprinted with permission of Circadian Information,www.circadian.com.)

daily sleep-wake cycles that alter our states of consciousness. Body temperatures, blood pressure, stress hormones, digestive secretions, and mental alertness all follow a daily pattern that resets itself according to daily cycles of sunlight and darkness. Of these, mental alertness may well be the most important to a diver, as it affects our decision-making ability.

According to experts in the field of circadian science, a person rising at 7:30 A.M. with adequate sleep will experience peak alertness levels in the morning around 8 to 9, and again in the evening between 7 and 9 (see FIGURE 4-2). Alertness drops to a lower level from about 12 noon to 3 P.M., and drops off rapidly after 9 P.M. Based on this data, divers can generally expect to have a reduced mental alertness for a late night dive. The excitement of a night dive might conspire to artificially elevate mental alertness during a night dive, but other factors including acute and chronic fatigue may also come into play.

The effects of fatigue on human performance have long been known and understood. Acute or short-term fatigue is the tiredness experienced after long periods of physical or mental strain. Extended periods of work, study, travel, physical exercise, or a lack of sleep can induce episodes of acute fatigue. The symptoms include reduced coordination and impaired alertness, both of which can be problems for divers. If a diver works, plays or parties too hard over a period of several days, the effects of acute fatigue can significantly degrade his performance and safety on a dive.

To illustrate the importance of mental alertness, consider the fact that 32 percent of marine accidents occur between the hours of 4 am and 8 am. It's also interesting to note that four of the worst industrial accidents in recent history involved impaired judgment caused by fatigue. The Chernobyl and Three Mile Island nuclear powerplant accidents, the grounding of the Exxon Valdez off the coast of Alaska, and the Bhopal, India chemical plant leak all occurred between midnight and 5 am—a period when mental alertness is at its lowest.

One approach to minimizing the effects of reduced mental alertness is to carefully plan and prepare for our night dives. By making our night dives relatively simple, and conducting them in low-risk environments, we can also reduce the potential for problems.

Circadian rhythms and fatigue aren't the only human factors challenges faced by night divers. Night diving also presents a number of physiological and biomechanical considerations including nutrition, night vision adaptation, heat balance, and increased task loading.

4.2 The Physiology of Night Diving

The night environment has a surprising number of physiological implications for the diver. Since we're conducting our dives late in the day, nutritional considerations become important. While our vision may adapt in part to the lower light levels, our perceptions also alter, creating new challenges to overcome. Our heat balance shifts from daytime diving, often causing us to become colder on a night dive. Finally, increased task-loading and biomechanical limitations may be a handicap when night diving, especially when complications arise.

4.2.1 Nutrition: A Diet for Night Diving

Nutrition is an important consideration for divers regardless of when they dive, but our nutritional strategy is particularly important at night when we strive to overcome the effects of circadian rhythms and fatigue.

Scientists and nutritionists have learned that good nutrition and eating habits play an important role in mental performance. The types of foods eaten and the sequence in which they are consumed have a marked impact on our state of mind, mental alertness, and reflexes.

Chemical neurotransmitters derived from the foods we eat help transmit messages to the brain, causing a response in terms of mental acuity and activity. Seratonin, a chemical neurotransmitter derived from carbohydrates, tends to have a calming, relaxing effect on mental activity. While this can help reduce stress, too much of a good thing can be bad as well. A high carbohydrate meal consisting of pasta, crepes, potatoes, starchy vegetables and sweets can increase seratonin levels enough to induce not just a pleasant feeling, but lethargy and the need to sleep. Likewise, fats tend to prolong digestion and rob the brain of blood to aid in the digestion process. The result is fatigue, sleepiness, and overall lack of alertness.

Alternatively, a meal that begins with high-protein foods such as steak, eggs, high protein cereals, and green beans, and is relatively low in carbohydrates and fat, will help promote mental alertness. Dopamine and norephinephrin, derived from protein in our food, stimulate the brain to higher levels of alertness and activity.

Most divers are savvy enough to avoid alcohol prior to a night dive. Alcohol affects both the central nervous system and the circulatory system in ways that can erode our margin of safety when diving. Even small amounts of alcohol have serious consequences for a diver.

First, alcohol adversely affects our central nervous system. Studies have shown that as little as one ounce of liquor, one bottle of beer, or four ounces of wine can degrade motor skills and impair judgment, and will be evident in the breath and blood for a period of at least three hours. There is evidence that alcohol also impairs our sleep, leaving us less rested after a night's sleep. Fatigue reduces our mental alertness and decision-making ability long after the direct effects of alcohol subside.

Alcohol causes a shift in blood circulation. Blood flow is increased to the surface of the skin while circulation to the tissues is reduced. The result is an increase in heat loss, as well as an increased predisposition to DCS.

Alcohol is a diuretic, and tends to dehydrate a diver. Dehydration reduces the blood's capacity to offgas nitrogen since blood flow is reduced throughout the tissues, thus increasing the risk of DCS.

Finally, alcohol alters the blood chemistry, which may increase the growth of microbubbles, thus leading to DCS. Researchers also have found that drinking increases oxygen consumption of the heart and other muscles during periods of exercise, so drinking may actually increase our air consumption. The bottom line is that if we're planning a dive after dark, it's best to stay away from the bar.

4.2.2 Night Vision Adaptation: Seeing Isn't Always Believing

As most divers would agree, the most obvious difference between a day dive and night dive is our inability to see as well at night. Ambient lighting in daylight allows us to see clearly, and our peripheral vision is limited only by the physical constraints of our mask. At night, the beam of our dive light limits our vision. This tends to focus our attention on a relatively small area of the submarine world, and has other consequences as well.

Surprisingly, we can often see significantly more than we might expect even without the aid of a dive light, although vision at night without artificial light may not be quite so clear. The retina of the human eye has two types of receptors, referred to as cones and rods. The cones are located in the central area of the retina and provide clear, focused vision in well-lighted conditions. The rods, located in the area surrounding the cones, see less clearly, but more readily adapt to dark lighting conditions.

Our best night vision develops after a period of exposure to low lighting, a process called dark adaptation. This can take as long as 30 minutes for total adaptation to blackness, but 20 minutes in dim red lighting will provide a moderate degree of adaptation. Dark adaptation is impaired by the carbon monoxide present in cigarette smoke, or a dive boat or compressor exhaust. If carbon monoxide finds it's way into our scuba cylinders, our night vision adaptation may be impaired, not to mention other serious side effects. Fatigue also degrades our visual sensitivity.

Even a brief exposure to white lights will require the lengthy adaptation process to restore night vision, so divers are reminded to be careful not to shine a dive light in another diver's eyes. Night vision may also be impaired for some time after submerging from a brightly lit environment.

Reduced visual perception can manifest additional problems on a night dive. Pilots have long been taught that various visual illusions, disorientation and vertigo can occur in a darkened environment. Our sense of balance and motion is derived from several sources, including visual references and the intricate mechanisms of the inner ear. Normally, our brain compares inputs from various senses to determine orientation and movement.

Without all the necessary information, the brain can become confused, causing the individual to take inappropriate actions. For example, certain accelerations caused by rapid head movement, turbulence or changes in aircraft orientation, combined with limited visual references can induce spatial disorientation or vertigo in pilots. If unaware of the problem, a pilot might put his aircraft in a dangerous position while attempting to rectify an incorrectly perceived problem. In these situations, pilots must rely on the aircraft instruments to determine the orientation and true motion of the aircraft. A failure to rely on or properly interpret flight instruments combined with the lack of visual references can cause a pilot to fly a perfectly good airplane into the ground.

For divers, a lack of visual references combined with rapid head movements, currents or surge can also create false perceptions of motion and orientation. Head first descents in dark or limited visibility water, even with a dive light, can result in disorientation and vertigo. When the beam of our dive light is scattered or reflected during a rapid descent, the effect can be similar to driving at night in a blinding snowstorm, and disorientation and vertigo can result. Failure to clear the ears frequently on descent, or unbalanced equalization between the two ears, can also contribute to the sensations of vertigo. To reduce the effect, make a slow, controlled, feet-first descent when diving from a boat or in open water. Following a descent line or anchor line and monitoring a depth gauge or computer during the descent virtually eliminates the vertigo and disorientation. Clearing the ears early and frequently will also help reduce the potential for vertigo.

Perhaps more importantly, a lack of visual references on the ascent can lead to disorientation and excessive ascent rates. Again, avoiding this problem on a night dive is relatively simple. On a shore dive, we can maintain contact with the bottom throughout a gradual, controlled ascent. When diving from a boat or surfacing in open water, a good option is to use an ascent line and closely monitor our depth gage or dive computer to maintain a proper ascent rate.

4.2.3 What's Hot and Who's Not: Night Shifts in the Diver's Heat Balance

While the water temperature might in fact be the same day or night, several factors may tend to increase our heat loss on a night dive. The air temperature is likely to be lower for a night dive than during the day, meaning our heat loss prior to and following a dive might be significantly greater. In addition, we have no sun to warm us before, between and after night dives.

TABLE 4-1 Effects of Low Body Core Temperature/ Hypothermia

Body Core Temperature		Indications
Degrees F	Degrees C	
98.6	37	Normal Temperature
95–98.6	35–37	Sensation of cold, increased heart rate, shivering, vasoconstriction, slight incoordination in hand movements, urge to urinate
90–95	32.2–35	Increased muscular incoordination, slurred speech, decreased or loss of shivering, weakness, apathy, drowsiness, confusion, impairment of rational thought
85–90	29.4–32.2	Loss of shivering, confusion progressing to coma, inability to follow commands, inappropriate behavior, loss of vision, temporary amnesia may occur, cardiac irregularities may develop

It's not unusual to begin a night dive with a heat deficit from the day's diving, particularly if we haven't taken the time to get the proper rest, warmth and nutrition following the day's diving. Experts warn us that it is quite possible to "feel" warm, even if our core temperature is reduced.

In his book *Deeper into Diving*, author and lecturer John Lippmann states, "Divers often disregard cumulative effects of repetitive diving. After the initial dive, the diver might experience superficial skin warming and thus feel warmer. However, his core temperature may still be reduced. Feeling warm is no guarantee that your heat losses have been replaced. The best way to show that your heat losses have been replaced is to start sweating. This shows the body needs to lose heat."

Don't make the mistake of considering heat loss as merely a matter of comfort. As with nutrition and fatigue, body temperature also has a direct effect on our mental processes. If our body temperature decreases significantly, our judgment might be jeopardized. In addition, our breathing rate may increase in response to cold, causing us to consume our air reserves more quickly.

"Cold induced mental changes are probably <u>the</u> danger to the diver," writes Lippmann, "because once the brain does not work properly, wrong decisions can easily be made. Some authorities believe that long, slow cooling of the body does not stimulate shivering and the subsequent heat re-generation. As a result, the diver might not notice the heat drain from his body until significant hypothermia has developed and shivering finally occurs. Some consider this 'silent hypothermia' to be the major hazard to the diver in cold water, as it will make the diver more accident-prone without him being aware of it."

The take-home message for night divers is to minimize heat loss. Precautions against heat loss may include wearing extra exposure protection on all dives prior to a night dive, even in warm waters. We can limit our cold exposure prior to night dives by limiting bottom time and depth. Limiting bottom time reduces the period during which the heat loss is high, and limiting depth minimizes the compression of the exposure suit, thus improving its performance. Changing into warm, dry clothing between dives can reduce evaporative cooling.

4.2.4 Task-Loading and the One-Handed Diver
Beyond the physiological considerations of a night dive, we must also contend with a basic biomechanical handicap. The simple act of using a hand-held dive light means that we have only one free hand. Buoyancy control, ear clearing, and communications must be accomplished "single-handed." While not necessarily a problem, the difficulty can increase dramatically when towing a surface float or manipulating other accessory equipment.

The single-hand limitation can become a significant handicap, even when contending with minor equipment problems. As distinguished researcher and author Dr. Glen Egstrom explains, "We typically use one hand to hold the dive light, and this becomes a problem in an emergency situation. If we drop the light so we can deal with the problem two-handed, we can no longer see."

Choosing a dive light with the proper characteristics can help solve the problem. The proper buoyancy, size and handle design may make a dive light easier to use, and thus ease the task loading associated with a night dive. Some divers find that a wrist mounted or head-mounted light reduces the workload and makes night diving easier. Another way to help cope with the problem of increased task loading during a night dive is to closely coordinate tasks with your buddy.

4.3 The Psychology of Night Diving

Divers are drawn to night diving like moths to a porch light, and there's really little surprise. Just the thought of venturing into the water at night can make your skin tingle with excitement. Entering a world illuminated only by our dive light, our attention is drawn to a sharp point of focus, and we find ourselves seeing the underwater world as if for the first time. "We have a entirely different psychological set at night," notes Egstrom. "First there's a peripheral narrowing that occurs as we increase the psychological stress. It becomes a more introverted dive, and this is actually something that people enjoy. The dive takes up more of our cognitive energy."

Indeed, there are stresses associated with a night dive. Perhaps the most obvious is the psychological stress of facing the unknown, and this can begin with the planning phase and continue throughout the entire dive. If we're unfamiliar with the area, with night diving procedures, or with the nature of marine life which might be encountered, our stress levels are certain to be heightened. Add unfamiliar equipment, a new or different buddy, or any other factors, and our baseline stress for a night dive can be significantly elevated.

While a low level of stress when diving can be helpful in focusing our attention on the situation at hand, too much stress can spell trouble. As stress increases further, our ability to maintain situational awareness decreases, degrading our ability to make the assessments necessary for safe, competent decision making. Increased stress may also translate to increased breathing rate, making air reserves a more critical consideration.

Human Factors and the Night Diver

A number of situations can arise on a night dive that bump up our stress level quite abruptly, especially if we're unprepared. One of the thrills of night diving is having unexpected sea creatures suddenly loom out of the darkness. But sometimes this surprise factor creates a momentary heightening of anxiety and stress. A minor equipment problem or disorientation can also spike our stress level until the situation is resolved.

The flip side to the enjoyable, introverted dive is a reduced situational awareness that erodes our decision-making ability. As Egstrom explains, "Since the peripheral visual field contracts during periods of increased stress, we lose a lot of information we might otherwise have." Sometimes divers become so engrossed with their surroundings at night that they fail to closely monitor their depth or air consumption.

The real problem comes when a situation begins to run awry. "At night, we might not be as likely to see a problem developing," suggests Egstrom. "So this narrowing of focus can be a problem when it comes to our buddy." If a situation is left unchecked, a full-blown emergency can develop, throwing divers into a dangerous spiral that runs out of control. An emergency that arises during the course of a night dive can elevate stress beyond the levels expected for a similar scenario in daylight. For example, a low air or out of air situation may be more stressful at night due to the difficulty of resolving the problem in darkness. The net result may be an inability to successfully complete a necessary task.

For this reason, divers must focus on situational awareness and keep tabs on their buddy during a night dive. By staying in a fixed position relative to one another, divers are less apt to become separated and can communicate more readily. By following such a protocol, the stresses that might develop can be minimized, and the potential for problems is greatly diminished.

4.4 Training and Fitness
The real keys to safe and enjoyable night diving are training and fitness. Proper training in night diving skills and procedures, combined with a regular program of fitness, form perhaps the

best strategy for mitigating any negative human factors considerations associated with night diving.

Night diver training focuses sharply on the night diving environment, skills, and the planning and preparation needed to safely conduct a night dive. The more we know about night diving and the environment in which we're diving, the more confidence we have in our abilities to dive safely. This confidence helps shield us against the effects of psychological stress.

Proper planning and preparation go a long way toward avoiding disorientation, vertigo, and potential emergencies. Start by preparing a detailed emergency procedures plan and review the elements of this plan before entering the water. The emergency plan should consider such contingencies as low air, out of air, entanglement, missing buddy, disorientation, a failed dive light(s), and other typical equipment problems.

To compensate for reduced mental alertness and the obvious difficulties of working in darkness, our strategy should be to prepare as much of our gear as practical during daylight hours when our mind is alert and it's easier to spot problems. This leaves only the process of suiting up and completing the necessary checks and safety briefings to be done prior to entering the water.

When an unplanned situation arises on a night dive, our response should be to stop, relax, breathe normally, and follow the established plan and procedures developed as part of the predive planning. If the situation lies beyond the established emergency plan, we must think rationally and communicate before launching into an action that might be unsafe.

A critical aspect of night diver training is practicing the requisite emergency skills and drills in a darkened environment. The need and use of dive lights, and the potential need to resolve a problem in near total darkness, often adds greater complexity to underwater emergency management, which requires additional practice to master.

Human Factors and the Night Diver

Handling a night diving emergency on the surface can be nearly as difficult as in the water. Hillary Viders is an international expert in emergency dive accident management who teaches Emergency Oxygen Administration and Dive Accident Management programs for the scuba, rescue and law enforcement industries. "When I teach professional rescuers," explains Viders, "I conduct a timed drill in which each team of four people has to assemble a complete oxygen kit from a pile of assorted components while administering CPR on an 'unconscious' victim. Usually a professional team (one who handles oxygen equipment and performs these tasks several times every day) can complete the drill in under 60 seconds. However, when I ask the same team to repeat the identical drill in a completely darkened room, it usually takes the best group at least five times longer, and some teams cannot do it correctly at all!"

Viders' experience underscores the need for thorough training and preparation in all aspects of night diving. Not only must in-water skills be practiced in the dark, but skills required to effectively manage a diving emergency must also be practiced under cover of darkness.

Good physical conditioning reduces the effort required to complete a dive, thus reducing the psychological stress. A high degree of fitness also allows us to perform better and for sustained periods when problems arise and during an emergency.

NOTES

CHAPTER 5

Night Diving Planning and Procedures

5.0 Primary Considerations

The keys to safe and successful night diving lie in thorough planning and adherence to established safe-diving procedures. An effective night dive plan will take into account the numerous factors discussed in the previous chapters. A thorough plan will also address all foreseeable complications, contingencies,

FIGURE 5-1 *(R.N. Rossier)*
Divers prepare for a night dive on the pier in Cozumel.

and emergencies, and spell out a planned response for each. Especially for a beginning night diver, you should start out by making low-stress night dives—dives conducted in well-known, shallow dive sites with clear waters and little or no current.

One way to acclimate to night diving is to participate in a dusk dive that ends after dark. Such a dive begins when there's plenty of natural light, and slowly evolves into a night dive. Many divers find that participating in such a dive alleviates their trepidations regarding night diving, and makes the transition to night diving less stressful.

5.0.1 Elements of Dive Planning

Dive plans, including those developed for a night dive, can vary dramatically in their complexity and detail. A dive plan for a night dive should be fairly comprehensive, especially when you're new to the activity. Some of the major elements in dive planning include:

(a) Objective—This is the reason for the dive. It can be as simple as observing the local aquatic or marine life, or as complicated as a wreck dive. The objective may be inextricably tied to the next element.

(b) Location—The particular dive site chosen for the dive can be broad and general, such as a reef area, bay or cove, or it can be a specific point such as a particular rock or wreck.

(c) Entry/Exit Points—These are the actual locations from which you will begin and end your dive, and their selection determines to a large degree the potential difficulty· or ease of the dive. A shore dive should have a primary and one or more alternate exit locations, depending on the dive site.

(d) Depth and Time—Every dive plan should establish limits on depth and time in order to avoid a decompression obligation. The depth of the dive site or the specific point of interest at the dive site often determines the depth. The time is determined primarily by the no-stop (no decompression) dive limits and air consumption.

(e) Air Consumption—Although actual air consumption will vary from diver to diver, it's important to establish a minimum reserve air pressure for any dive. The necessary reserve is based on the type of dive and the environment. A dive that requires a return underwater swim may impose a greater air reserve. Difficult exits and potential for entanglements will also necessitate a greater air reserve. Generally, divers choose a minimum air reserve of between 500 and 1,000 psi.

(f) Navigation—The navigation component of the dive may also be simple or complex, depending on how difficult it is to find the underwater objective and return to the exit point. Surface and underwater navigation may include a variety of techniques including compass bearings, natural navigation, the use of range or marker lights, and any number of electronic navigation devices.

(g) Procedures and Protocols—The procedures and protocols defined by the dive plan are derived from various training programs and applied or adapted to the specific environment and dive objectives. Procedures and protocols include a myriad of considerations including equipment preparation, entries and exits, underwater communications, and the preparation and application of special equipment, to name a few.

(h) Contingencies—This part of our dive plan establishes the protocols we'll follow in the event that something goes wrong during the dive. In some cases, the protocols are the same regardless of the dive. In other cases, the location and resources dictate the manner in which particular problems will be resolved. Typical contingencies include everything from light failure, out-of-air scenarios and separated buddies to jellyfish stings, decompression illness, and emergency evacuations.

(i) Special Equipment—The other planning elements often determine special equipment requirements. Special equipment could include anything from special lights, surface floats and lift bags to GPS navigation equipment, portable compressors and air testing equipment.

(j) Communications—The final element of the dive plan is communications, which encompasses everything from hand signs, to light signals, to cellular service, marine radiotelephone procedures and emergency phone numbers. While much of the communications element is common to most dives, the location often determines the topside communications options.

5.0.2 Personal Readiness
Personal readiness is an important safety consideration for any dive, but it takes on added importance for a night dive. Before undertaking a night dive, take the steps necessary to insure that you're well rested, warm, and have eaten properly. Always avoid alcohol prior to night diving. One way to assess your personal fitness is with the I'M SAFE checklist. This is an acronym that stands for Illness, Medication, Stress, Alcohol, Fatigue and Eating (nutrition). If you find yourself deficient in any of these categories, put off diving until another time. For more information on self-assessment for diving, consult *Dive Like a Pro: 101 Ways to Improve Your Diving Skills and Safety* (available from Best Publishing Company).

Personal readiness also implies the proper skills and training. Before taking on a night dive, you should be properly certified, have recent diving experience, and be competent with all the basic diving skills including buoyancy control, mask clearing, ascents and descents, and emergency procedures.

5.1 Site Selection
The first step in planning a night dive is choosing an appropriate dive site. If possible, choose a site with which you're already familiar. If you haven't been diving at the particular site before, consider making a daytime dive there to increase your familiarity and assess any potential risks and hazards. In clear waters, even snorkeling the site in daylight can improve your familiarity.

5.1.1 Entry and Exit Considerations
A primary consideration for a night dive from shore is the location(s) for entry and exit to the water. Attempting to negotiate a difficult entry or exit can be much more difficult at night. Be sure to identify any obstacles, as well as the surface conditions. An area of slippery rocks, particularly when combined with surf

FIGURE 5-2
Slippery rocks with strong surge and surf are a hazardous combination for a night dive.

(R.N. Rossier)

and darkness, can be a particularly hazardous combination. Also, consider the effects of tides, windy conditions or high surf on the entry and exit locations. A good dive site will have protected areas where safe entries and exits can be made even in moderate sea conditions.

For all dives, but particularly those where currents can be a factor, have one or more alternate exit locations. It may not be practical or possible for divers to return to the primary exit location if a current carries them too far, or if problems develop that require an expeditious exit from the water.

5.1.2 Identifying Underwater Hazards
As part of the site evaluation, identify all potential underwater hazards. Consider factors that might affect visibility, such as a bottom composed of fine silt or sediment, or nearby streams or rivers that could bring turbid waters following a rainy period.

Also note any potential entanglement hazards, including fishing lines and abandoned nets. Particularly in rivers or areas with currents, submerged trees can cause a serious entanglement hazard.

Overhead environments—including caves, caverns, ice, wrecks, and kelp—should be strictly avoided on night dives unless all divers are trained, certified and experienced in those environments. In dark conditions, a diver may not at first realize he is entering a cave or cavern, and darkness adds a greater degree of difficulty in negotiating the hazards of other overhead environments.

Finally, consider any forms of marine life that could cause problems, from barnacle covered rocks on the entry, to stinging jellyfish and other species, to large marine predators such as tiger sharks. Heavy boat traffic, such as in a channel used both in daylight and at night, is another potential risk that should be carefully evaluated.

5.1.3 Navigation Considerations
As part of your site evaluation process, consider any factors that may affect navigation. Currents can pose a potential problem in terms of navigation, so be sure to consider their effects. When surveying the site, take note of any features that may aid in underwater navigation, as well as navigation on the surface. Keep in mind that natural navigation can be more difficult at night since the diver can only see what lies directly in his beam of light.

Check the area at night and make note of any existing surface lights that may aid or confuse nighttime navigation. As part of a night beach dive plan, you'll be determining the location(s) for position or range lights to be used to navigate back to the exit point, and existing lighting and terrain features may influence the positioning of these lights. Be particularly leery of lights that turn on and off automatically, or that may be turned on or off by someone other than a member of your dive party.

5.2 Evaluating Conditions

So far, we've looked at the general factors that make a site suitable or unsuitable for a night dive. Once a site has been selected and a time determined for the dive, it's time to evaluate the specific environmental conditions anticipated for the dive. If conditions are unfavorable, reschedule the dive or choose an alternative location.

A number of weather conditions, either existing or forecast, may force you to reschedule your night dive. High winds, cold temperatures, heavy rain, thunderstorms or fog should all be considered contraindications to safe recreational night diving.

High winds may have several negative effects, including the development of high seas, pounding surf, and powerful surge. For a boat dive, high winds may make it difficult or impossible for divers to safely gear up and enter or exit the water. High winds may make it more difficult to anchor or moor the boat, and a diver who surfaces away from the boat may be quickly swept further from safety or out of sight.

FIGURE 5-3   *(R.N. Rossier)*
The approach of inclement weather, clearly seen in daylight, may be invisible at night.

Diving into Darkness

Cold temperatures can increase the heat loss of divers as they prepare for their dive, leading to impaired physical (or mental) performance on the dive. Heavy rain or fog can make it difficult or impossible for divers (or the skipper of the dive boat) to see important visual references needed to navigate on the surface. Thunderstorms pose a myriad of serious threats, including rough water conditions, high winds, rain, hail, and the potential for lightning strikes.

Also look at the existing and forecast sea conditions, recognizing that these are often determined by weather conditions that otherwise have no local impact. High surf and surge can be caused by weather conditions hundreds of miles away, even when local winds are light and sky conditions clear.

Tides may also be an important factor to consider. Tides may dramatically alter the entry and exit locations, particularly in higher latitudes. Visibility can also be impacted by the tide.

When assessing currents, remember that these are often related to tidal movements, and may be influenced by the lunar cycle. Tide charts and other local information can be useful in predicting the strength and direction of currents for a particular day and time. If strong currents are anticipated, it's best to consider an alternative day or time for the dive. At the very least, you may want to alter your dive plan, taking into account the effects of currents.

In summary, the best and safest conditions for a night dive include clear, relatively calm weather with minimal surf, surge and currents.

5.3 Predive Equipment Preparation

Rule number one of night dive equipment preparation is to gear up as much as practical in daylight. It's much easier to set up your equipment when you can see it well, and you'll be more likely to detect any problems that might be overlooked in dim lighting. Plan your dive schedule to take advantage of full lighting to initially set up your gear.

In addition to your dive gear, be sure to test all emergency and first aid equipment, and lay it out or stow it in an easily accessible manner. This includes emergency breathing oxygen, first aid kits, informational resources such as books and emergency flow charts, and emergency lighting.

Of course, final preparations and suiting up must be done just prior to the dive. Instead of using your dive light for this step, have another flashlight or lantern available. As an alternative, floodlights on the deck of a boat or at the shore-side location can aid in the final steps of preparation.

Be sure to conduct a predive equipment check before entering the water. To conserve battery power for the dive, use a light other than your dive light. In addition to the normal predive checks, test each of your lights to be certain that they are accessible and functioning. You should be able to locate and detach your backup light(s) by feel alone.

FIGURE 5-4
A cardinal rule in night diving is to prepare your equipment in bright daylight.

(R.N. Rossier)

We usually anticipate a higher breathing rate for a night dive than for a daytime dive. The psychological stresses, anticipation, and excitement often translate to a higher breathing rate, but other factors can also come into play. For example, cold stress can increase our breathing rate as our body attempts to compensate. To minimize this effect, wear sufficient clothing to stay warm during the transit to the dive site and during the initial stages of preparation.

5.4 Preparing the Dive Site

Whether you're planning a night dive from a boat or from shore, an important part of the plan includes preparing the site for your dive.

5.4.1 Boat Dive

If you're fortunate enough to be making a dive from a boat, the process of setting up should be relatively easy. A boat properly equipped for night diving will have sufficient deck lighting to allow you to complete the final assembly of your gear, and to suit up and perform necessary buddy checks. An anchor light or illuminated dive flag will assist you in identifying the boat at the end of the dive.

It's a good idea to attach some form of marker or strobe light to aid in navigation back to the down line or anchor line. The particular environment (depth, visibility, seafloor topography, etc.) will determine the best placement for the marker/strobe lights. In some instances, more than one light may be desired to ensure positive navigation.

5.4.2 Shore Dive

When making a night dive from shore, set up your equipment much the same as you do for daytime dives, using tarps or other appropriate surfaces on which to sort out your gear, don your equipment, and repack your gear at the end of the dive. Some broad beam lighting (flood lights) will be very helpful for all these activities, as well as to provide lighting necessary to administer first aid to an injured diver.

While it may be possible to use existing shore lighting to navigate back to shore at the end of the dive, remember that you don't have control over the operation of these lights. Lights that automatically or otherwise turn on or off can significantly alter the appearance of the shoreline from the water. A better approach is to set up some sort of navigation lighting to serve this function.

One form of navigation lighting, often referred to as range lights, is used to guide divers back to shore along a particular bearing or course. Range lights are usually placed near the shore, with one slightly higher and well behind the other. Divers on the surface can swim parallel to the shore until the two lights line up, then swim straight toward the lights to maintain the proper course (see FIGURE 5-5). Position lights can be used to mark the exit location for the dive.

When selecting the location of navigation lights, take into consideration surrounding lights. A well-lit background may make it difficult to distinguish the navigation lights. Also of primary importance is to not use a light that may be confused with marine navigation lights. Red and green lights should generally be avoided, and some strobes may also be confusing

FIGURE 5-5
Range lights are used to guide divers back along a predetermined course clear of obstacles to the exit point on shore.

to boaters. Check with local authorities before setting up navigation lights.

It's also important to position night diving navigation lights so they are not behind obstacles, and can be readily seen from the surface. This is usually checked prior to the night dive, and rechecked by the first divers heading out to make their dive.

5.5 Communication

Communications are perhaps even more important at night than during a daytime dive, and the process of communicating is complicated by darkness. While some signals can be done with the light itself, divers typically must hold a dive light in one hand, and shine it on the hand with which they are signing.

While some light signals are standard among many divers and agencies, there are differences. Be sure to review hand signals with your buddy as well as with boat crew or friends on shore with whom you may need to communicate. Some of the more common light signals are identified in TABLE 5-1 below.

Above all, avoid shining your dive light into the eyes of another diver. Doing so may temporarily blind a diver, degrading their night vision, and perhaps putting them in a foul mood.

Other forms of communication can also be implemented on a night dive. While it may be cumbersome without a head-mounted light, an underwater slate can be used to communicate messages that are more complex. An underwater rattle, tank tapper, or knife banging on your cylinder can be an excellent way to get the attention of your buddy or other divers in the water.

Various methods can also be used to attract attention and communicate while on the surface. When boat diving, it may be necessary to attract the attention of the boat crew and signal for a pickup at the end of the dive. Shining your dive light at the vessel is a good way to attract attention. You can also use your light to illuminate your face, or to illuminate a safety sausage. In some

TABLE 5-1 Common Light Signals for Night Diving

Message	Light Signal
OK	Rotate light in a circular motion
Attention	Slowly move light side to side in your buddy's view
Emergency	Rapidly move light up and down in your buddy's view

circles, a light held overhead shining down on you is another "OK" signal. Some divers may utilize other means, such as a personal strobe, to make themselves more visible to the boat crew. Just be sure not to use a light source on your boat or buoy that could be misidentified by boaters as a navigational light.

Regardless of which means you choose, make certain that your communication protocol has been reviewed with the boat crew (safety personnel) and other divers. Some operators request that divers not shine their lights on the surface except in an emergency.

5.6 Entries and Descents

Entering the water at night requires a bit more care than daytime entries to avoid such problems as disorientation and vertigo. Especially when making a boat dive, divers should be certain to turn on their primary dive light prior to entering the water. This will ensure that the light is working, and make it easy to locate should it become separated from you during the entry.

To avoid disorientation and vertigo, a feet-first descent is recommended. Remember to stop and clear your ears frequently to avoid the pain and disturbances to your equilibrium. It's best to use a down line or the anchor line to measure your descent and maintain a fixed visual reference. A rapid, head-first descent, especially when shining your light ahead of you, can induce vertigo. Plankton, particulates and other matter in the water is reflected by your light, creating an effect similar to driving into a blinding snowstorm. If you begin to get disoriented, watch your bubbles to determine which way is up.

When beginning the dive from shore, turn on your light before entering the water, and make your way slowly and carefully into the water. When you've reached water of sufficient depth, submerge and follow the bottom to make a gradual descent. If you must make a surface swim before submerging, you'll need to make a gradual, feet-first descent. A line and surface float can be used to provide a reference and make a controlled descent.

5.7 Night Navigation
Although navigation at a night dive can be more challenging in some respects, the proper lighting techniques and attention to detail goes a long way to overcoming the problems. First, always

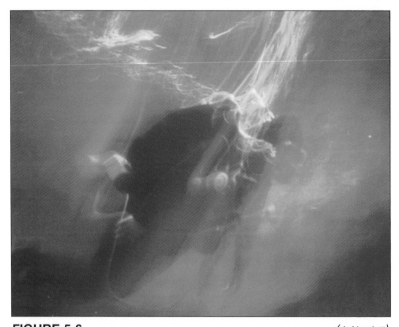

FIGURE 5-6   (*J. Hewlett*)
A number of techniques can be used to avoid disorientation and vertigo while night diving.

use a compass, and take accurate bearings to the shore references before submerging. It's very easy on a night descent to get turned around, so once you're on the bottom, check your compass again to be certain of your orientation prior to swimming. You may want to attach a marker strobe to the bottom or the boat's anchor to help you get back to your starting point, especially if you plan to use the anchor line as an ascent line. A marker strobe secured to the bottom can also be important if you plan to follow a compass bearing from that point back to your shore exit.

Although it is more difficult to pick out references on a night dive due to the limited illumination of your dive light, natural navigation techniques can be useful on a night dive. Sand ripples, depth contours, and other notable features can often be used successfully at night. Still, a good plan is to back up your natural navigation with compass navigation. Some divers also find that electronic underwater navigation systems are particularly helpful at night.

When using a compass at night, be careful not to hold a powerful light too close to your compass. The magnetic field created by the light's electrical circuit can deflect the needle on your compass quite significantly. This effect can be tested before using a particular light and compass combination.

Take note of the effects of any current or surge as you begin your dive, and monitor your drift throughout the dive. It's best to start your dive against the current, and then use the current to help carry you back to your starting point.

Maintaining buddy contact during the dive is important to safety in many regards. Besides having a buddy at-the-ready in the event of an emergency, staying in proper position during the dive can make other activities, such as navigation, much simpler. One approach to this is to adopt the leader/wingman configuration. The leader stays slightly ahead and to one side of the wingman, and performs the duties of navigation. The wingman stays in position slightly behind and to the side of the leader. Just be certain to agree on the position—wingman to the left or right—prior to the dive, and maintain the same position through-out the dive. If this convention is followed, each diver will always know exactly where the other one is throughout the dive.

Throughout the dive, be certain to monitor your depth and air consumption, and stick to the limitations established in your dive plan.

5.8 Ascent and Exit
The ascent and exit from a night dive are often some of the most difficult parts of the dive. Following the bottom contours along a predetermined compass course to a shore exit to make a slow ascent is perhaps the easiest, since you maintain a fixed visual reference throughout the ascent. If you must make a deep-water ascent, use an anchor line, ascent line, surface float line, or lift bag and reel to maintain a reference during the ascent. Maintaining a maximum 30-foot per minute ascent rate and making a 15-foot safety stop will help keep the ascent con-trolled and reduces the potential risks of DCS.

During your exit from the water, use the light to avoid obsta-cles, and keep it turned on until you reach a point where you can see without it. To avoid losing your light, do not turn it off until you are completely out of the water. Again, if you begin to get disoriented, watch your bubbles to determine which way is up.

5.9 Safety Personnel
An important ingredient for any night dive is personnel at the surface to oversee the safety of the dive. While it isn't necessary that these individuals be divers, they should be well versed in diving operations, and trained in managing diving accidents. Prior to the dive, the safety personnel must be informed of the dive plan (especially bottom time), and protocols for dealing with a wide variety of potential problems should be reviewed. Such problems should include medical problems, failure of navigation lights, use of alternative exit locations, and assisting or retriev-ing disabled or disoriented divers on the surface.

Always have at least one person on board the boat at all times for a night dive. This person or boat crew should be competent in boat handling, and able to monitor the position of the boat and make certain the anchor doesn't drag. They will also ensure that lights are operating so that the divers can find their way back to the boat. With the approach or onset of inclement weather or other problems, the boat crew can sound the recall signal to get the divers back on board. Finally, the boat crew can help deal with any form of emergency that may arise, initiating calls for emergency assistance, conducting searches, assisting divers on board and administering first aid.

Similarly for a shore dive, the safety personnel will monitor the operation of the navigation lights, and assist in any emergency that may arise during the course of the dive. Should divers experience difficulties, the safety personnel can initiate emergency communication, assist in guiding divers to alternate exit locations, help divers out of the water, and administer first aid.

5.10 Night Diving Emergencies
A critical element in any night diver training program is learning to deal with emergency situations. During this phase of the training, divers are taught the protocols for dealing with numerous situations. Since there may be differences in the specific procedures taught by various instructors and certification agencies, it's important to review the specific procedures prior to diving. In spite of any differences in specific procedures, many common elements are shared throughout the night diving community.

Key elements in managing an underwater emergency include knowing the remedial procedure and having practiced the procedure frequently. Knowing what procedure to follow and following it promptly limits the in-water stress and decision-making requirements that can lead to panic.

Although we normally use dive lights on all our night dives, an important point to remember is that we can function without them. Virtually all the tasks we may be called upon to perform in the water can be accomplished with little or no lighting. At the beginning of each dive, turn off your light and take note of the degree of illumination. Even after just a few minutes of adaptation, you may be surprised to see just how much natural light from the moon and stars, as well as manmade lighting, is available. We can often see quite well with natural lighting alone.

Still, resolving a diving emergency at night is often more stressful than dealing with the same problem during the day. By practicing the skills regularly, and reviewing the emergency procedures prior to the dive, you will be better prepared to handle the real situation when it arises.

5.10.1 Light Failure
The most obvious emergency on a night dive is failure of a dive light. If a light floods, immediately switch to your backup, turn off the flooded light and secure it to a D-ring or other suitable location. If a light should fail during a night dive, you should stop, secure the light, and switch to a backup light. Again, keep your backup light(s) in an easily accessible location, and turn it on before you unclip it for use. In the event that your fumble and drop it, you'll be able to find it if it's turned on.

When one diver in the team no longer has a backup light, it's time to call the dive. For this reason, many night divers carry two or more backup lights. A spare light is a small price to pay compared to the cost in time and money of making a night dive.

5.10.2 Lost/Separated Buddy
Equally as stressful a situation is a lost buddy scenario on a night dive. If this occurs, stop, cover your light, and use an audible signal to gain his attention. Then make a slow 360-degree turn to search for your buddy. With luck, you should be able to find him from the glow of his light. If you don't find your buddy within one minute, begin your ascent and locate him at the surface. If your buddy does not immediately appear at the surface, search the water surface for bubbles (if surface conditions make this possible) or an emergency buoy. If your buddy still cannot be found, immediately signal for help.

If you become separated from your buddy and cannot ascend for some reason (i.e. entanglement), above all remain calm.

Send your emergency ascent lift bag, attached to your line reel, to the surface. Rescuers at the surface should quickly determine you are missing and initiate a search.

5.10.3 Disorientation and Vertigo

Vertigo is a condition in which a diver perceives motion, but is unable to determine the direction or speed of movement. Vertigo can cause disorientation, dizziness, and even nausea. A number of factors can induce vertigo in a diver. Cold water entering the external ear canal can induce a condition of imbalance leading to vertigo. The condition may last until the water has been warmed by body heat. Pressure imbalances between the left and right ear during descent can also cause vertigo. Disorientation and vertigo can occur at night when a diver has no visual references to determine orientation or motion.

Divers can often overcome the effects of disorientation and vertigo by following standard procedures at the onset of the condition. As with all problems and potential emergencies that arise underwater, divers must remember to stop, breathe, think, and then act. When disorientation occurs, refer to your compass and depth gauge to reorient yourself. Holding onto one's self or buddy until the vertigo passes can also be helpful.

Remember, too, that bubbles go up. Shine your dive light to illuminate your bubbles as an additional reference. If you can't see your bubbles, put your hand near your regulator exhaust and feel their direction of movement

5.10.4 Out-of-Air

An out-of-air situation at night is doubly difficult. First, the stress is often higher due to the dark environment, but more important is the fact that you're short handed. In a normal air-share situation, you may have been taught to hold onto your buddy with your left hand. This stabilizes your positions and leaves your right hand available to switch regulators and manage buoyancy for the ascent.

At night, if you're using a hand-held light, the task is more complicated. It may be necessary to hold your light and your buddy with the same hand. If you can't manage holding onto your light while air sharing, consider clipping the light to a D-ring and leaving it turned on. Although the light won't be shining where you need it, the illumination may still be useful. Switching to a smaller backup light may be another alternative. Using a head or wrist-mounted light will free up your hands and be a tremendous help in virtually any emergency situation. A small light clipped to a convenient location on your BC can also provide necessary illumination in an emergency.

With the proper training and practice, you should be able to accomplish an air-sharing ascent even without an operating dive light. Just remember that the added stress of a real emergency may push some divers closer to panic, making it difficult to follow the established air-share game plan in darkness.

FIGURE 5-7
A backup light with a wrist lanyard is quickly configured as a wrist-mounted light to free a hand when dealing with problems on a night dive.

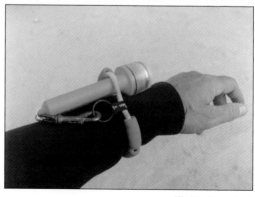

(R.N. Rossier)

92

Practicing the procedure in a controlled environment under the supervision of an experienced instructor can help prepare for such a high-stress situation.

Maintaining a slow, controlled ascent is critical in an air-sharing situation. Even without a light, luminescent gauges, display backlighting, or specialty gauge lights should be adequate for you to monitor your depth and ascent rate without the aid of a dive light.

Regardless of the protocol planned for a night air-sharing scenario, be sure to practice the procedure before diving to work out the bugs.

5.10.5 Beyond the Limits

Sticking to your dive plan is important, but sometimes a situation runs awry, pushing you past the planned depth or time limits. If this should happen on a night dive, follow the same protocol established for daytime dives. If you've exceeded the no-stop limits, extend the length of your safety stop, using as much air as practical. Once you're on the surface, notify your buddies or group leader, and take the appropriate steps. The use of oxygen may be beneficial even if no symptoms arise, and should always be initiated as soon as possible following the onset of any suspicious symptoms. Seek medical attention even if symptoms are relieved after using oxygen.

5.10.6 Medical Emergencies

Most problems that arise in the water must be dealt with in the water, but some will require treatment once the diver exits the water. These include DCS and marine life injuries. Any suspected DCS symptoms should be first treated using portable oxygen. Beyond that, divers should follow the established protocols and pursue prompt medical treatment. Numerous books and articles have been published which can skillfully guide the diver through the process of providing first aid, and such information is beyond the scope of this book. For more information and to obtain real-time medical advice, divers are encouraged to contact the Divers Alert Network. Since marine life injuries are more likely on a night dive than during the daylight hours, basic information on the treatment of some such injuries is included in Appendix A.

5.11 Summary: Night Diving Planning and Precautions

Night diving isn't unduly complicated, but it does require a modicum of training beyond basic open water diving. Before attempting a night dive, be certain to receive the proper training. The following planning tips and precautions can help make your night diving safer and more enjoyable.

1) Always evaluate a dive site in daylight before attempting a night dive. The evaluation should include, but not be limited to, safe entry and exit locations, potential hazards (including entanglements), currents, navigation features, and forecast weather conditions. Familiarity with the dive site reduces the psychological stress of a night dive, allowing divers to better focus on other safety concerns throughout the dive.

2) Avoid night diving in conditions of foul weather (including forecast fog or heavy rain), high seas, strong surf, strong currents, or unreasonable entanglement hazards. Such conditions pose an unnecessary risk to diver safety. Also avoid overhead environments, including kelp, at night until you accumulate the requisite experience to do so safely.

3) Enjoy a good meal prior to a night dive, but avoid consumption of alcohol.

4) Don't dive unless you're well rested and warm. If necessary, limit your daytime diving in order to be better prepared for a night diving excursion. An afternoon nap, even if it's only 15–20 minutes long, may leave you feeling more rested and improve your alertness for a night dive. Mild exercise can help restore the heat deficit from daytime diving.

5) Proper site preparation is key to all night dives. Surface navigation lights, working lights, emergency first aid

equipment, communication equipment, and rescue gear should all be properly set up prior to entering the water. Always have at least one person remaining at the surface or on the boat to deal with problems such as failed surface navigation lights and dragging anchors. This individual should also be prepared to deal with emergencies, and to call for assistance if necessary.

6) Always begin a night dive with at least two dive lights per diver. If a dive light fails, the dive can be safely completed and terminated with the extra light. For hands-free night diving, consider using a wrist-mounted or head-mounted dive light as a primary dive light.

7) To ease the psychological stress of night diving, instructors and new night divers should consider starting the first night dive at dusk. This is much less intimidating for the novice diver as the underwater world slowly fades from light to dark. A light isn't even necessary at the beginning of the dive, but is turned on as darkness fills the water.

8) While night diving emergencies are part of every night dive plan, few divers actually practice emergency procedures at night. To keep your skills sharp, confidence high, and stress reduced, practice night diving emergency skills regularly. Many skills can be accomplished in a pool, and others can be practiced safely in open water. If you haven't practiced night diving emergency skills in the open water lately, have an instructor guide you through the proper exercises.

NOTES

Appendix A

Stickers, Stingers, and Nighttime Zingers: Treating Common Night Diving Stings and Stabs

Note: The information provided in this appendix constitutes a brief introduction to the topic. The reader is encouraged to obtain additional formal training and instruction in treatment of marine life injuries. Additional references pertaining to this topic are provided in Appendix B.

According to sources at the Divers Alert Network, more than 50 million jellyfish stings occur annually worldwide, with more than 10 million stings occurring in the U.S. Four species are capable of inflicting fatal stings in humans. These are the Portuguese man-of-war, found along the southeastern U.S. Atlantic coast; two species of the box jelly found in the Indo-Pacific from Okinawa to Australia and along the Gulf coast of Texas; and the Stomolphus nomuri found in China's Yellow Sea. Surprisingly, only about two deaths per year occur, usually in small children.

Jellyfish are often seen on night dives, so divers should take precautions to avoid contact, especially unprotected areas such as the face or hands. If stings occur, administer basic first aid, and seek immediate medical attention.

Basic first aid for jellyfish stings begins with stabilizing the victim's vital signs. First check the ABC's—airways, breathing, and circulation—providing CPR or resuscitation if required.

Keep the injured diver quiet and comfortable. The stings are very painful, and muscular activity only serves to circulate the venom through the body in larger doses. Analgesics can be used to reduce the pain. If a box jellyfish stung the diver, the antivenin should be administered as soon as possible.

Next, neutralize the stingers. Many stingers may be left on the skin, and unless removed or neutralized, will continue to break and sting, especially if rubbed. Applying white vinegar in liberal amounts or a 50/50 mixture of water and baking soda on the affected area will neutralize the stinging nematocysts. In the waters of the Gulf coast of Texas and the Atlantic coast south of Chesapeake Bay, vinegar is the first choice. North of the Chesapeake Bay and in the central and northern Pacific regions, apply a thin coating of the 50/50 baking soda and water mixture. If you don't have vinegar or baking soda, irrigate the affected area with saline solution. While some experts recommend irrigation with seawater if saline is not available, others warn against the practice if the victim has open wounds, as seawater may be laden with potentially harmful marine bacteria.

Once you've neutralized the stingers, remove any remaining tentacles with forceps or tweezers. Shaving the area with shaving cream and a safety razor can also help remove remaining stingers.

Finally, apply hydrocortisone cream or lotion and monitor for allergic reactions and/or infections. Application of ice packs can also help relieve the discomfort.

If you're the one providing first aid, be sure to take the proper precautions to avoid getting stung yourself. A pair of protective medical gloves is recommended.

Another common night diving injury comes in the form of sea urchin punctures. Most spines are solid with a blunt tip, but others are hollow with a sharp tip. The spines contain venom that can include a neurotoxin and/or a cardiovascular toxin. Wearing booties and exercising caution during entries and exits, along with careful buoyancy control, go a long way toward avoid these maladies.

When a puncture occurs, only minor pain is initially perceived. Within 15 to 30 minutes, the pain intensifies and can last several hours.

There's a broad variation in the long range of effects of an urchin spine puncture. The symptoms may spontaneously resolve in a few weeks, with the broken spine remnants being absorbed or extruded from the skin. In rare cases, a diver may experience nausea, respiratory distress, muscle weakness, inability to control voluntary muscle movements, fainting or lightheadedness, or prickling and tingling skin. A secondary infection may also result from the wound. In some cases, delayed skin reactions can develop months after the injury, appearing as firm, flesh colored or purple nodules in the skin.

If the spine punctures a small joint, a condition called tenosynovitis—an inflammation of the joint tendons and joint space lining—may develop. Tenosynovitis causes the joint to become red, swollen and painful, and can result in a long-term loss of joint function.

Home medicine mythology includes a variety of treatments for urchin spine punctures, none of which are supported by scientific data. These include washing the wound with urine or ammonia, applying hot mud, poultices or skin softeners.

If a diver does receive a spine puncture, the first aid treatment should again begin with stabilizing the patient's vital functions. Once the condition is stabilized, gently remove the fragile spine fragments with forceps or tweezers. Rinse the wound with fresh water or saline solution. Immersion in hot water (113°F/45C maximum) for 30 to 90 minutes or the use of heat packs can help deactivate the venom. Pain can be treated with analgesics, and antibiotics used to fight infections. Particularly if a joint is punctured, or neurological or cardiovascular symptoms develop, seek immediate medical attention.

More information on the treatment of marine life injuries can be found in the references cited in Appendix B. For immediate medical assistance with stings, punctures, and other diving medical emergencies, contact the Divers Alert Network diving emergency hotline at 919-684-8111.

NOTES

Appendix B: Key References and Resources

Marine Weather/Oceanography/Boating

"A Change in the Weather Service," U.S. Department of Commerce, National Oceanic and Atmospheric Administration, Nov. 1993.

"A Mariner's Guide to Weather Services," U.S. Department of Commerce, National Oceanic and Atmospheric Administration, National Weather Service, NOAA/PA 92056.

Chapman Piloting, *Seamanship, and Small Boat Handling*, William Morrow and Company, NY, 1989.

Darcy, Michael P., "Don't Be Shocked," *Cruising World*, April 1994.

Rossier, Robert N., "Where Lightning Strikes," *Private Pilot Magazine*, Aug. 1992.

"Safe Boating Weather Tips," U.S. Department of Commerce, National Oceanic and Atmospheric Administration, National Weather Service NOAA/PA 94058.

"Thunderstorms and Lightning...the Underrated Killers," U.S. Department of Commerce, National Oceanic and Atmospheric Administration, Jan. 1994.

U.S. Coast Guard Auxiliary, *Boating Skills and Seamanship*, Hearst Corporation.

United States Power Squadron, *United States Power Squadron's Boating Course*, Hearst Marine Books, NY, 1989.

Van Dorn, William G., *Oceanography and Seamanship*, Dodd, Mead and Company, NY, 1974.

Rossier, Robert N., "A Prescription for Curiosity: Oceanography for Divers" *Dive Training Magazine*, June 1994.

Marine Life/Marine Ecology

Cancelmo, Jesse, "Night Moves: Coral Spawning by the Light of the Moon," *Dive Training Magazine*, Aug. 2000.

Cundiff, Mel, Ph.D., Professor of Biology, University of Colorado, Boulder, CO, "Scuba Diving at Night—General Information," Unpublished, personal communication, Spring 2000.

Cundiff, Mel, Ph.D., "Biological Diversity in Cozumel Marine Waters," Coral Reef Ecology Course, University of Colorado, Boulder, CO.

Burgess, George H. and Mathew Callahan, "Shark Attack on Divers: How Great the Risk?" International Shark Attack Files, Florida Museum of Natural History, University of Florida, Gainesville, FL, 1995.

Litteral, Linda Lambert, Ed. D., "By Dawn's Early Light: Some of the Best Night Dives Aren't Always at Night," *Dive Training Magazine*, Nov. 1995.

Martin, Richard, *Shark Smart,* Diving Naturalist Press, North Vancouver, British Columbia, 1995.

Nord, Dan, "Predator Provocation," *Alert Diver Magazine*, July/Aug. 1998.

Rossier, Robert N., "Swimming With Sharks," *Dive Training Magazine*, Mar. 1996.

Rossier, Robert N., "Shark Avoidance," *Alert Diver Magazine*, July/Aug. 1998.

Scarr, Dee, "Night Diving—The Really Unusual," *Dive Training Magazine*, July 1997.

Scarr, Dee, "Dusk Diving—Get Ready for Secrets of a Twilight Dive," *Dive Training Magazine*, May, 1997.

Sisto, Dawn Terlesky, Ed., *Aquarium of the Americas Naturalist Guide Training Manual*, Aquarium of the Americas, New Orleans, LA, 1992.

Night Diving Equipment

Laymon, Lynn, "Real-Life Uses for Dive Reels," *Dive Training Magazine*, May 2000.

Rossier, Robert N., "Let it Shine," *Alert Diver Magazine*, July/Aug. 1996.

Rossier, Robert N., "Summoning Assistance," *Alert Diver Magazine*, Sep./Oct. 1996.

Rossier, Robert N., "Light up Your Dive: A Guide to Underwater Lights," *Dive Training Magazine*, Oct. 1997.

Rossier, Robert N., "Let's Get Reel: Here's the Straight Scoop on Lines and Handling Devices," *Alert Diver Magazine*, May/June 1999.

Human Factors

Bachrach, Arthur J. and Glen H. Egstrom, *Stress and Performance in Diving*, Best Publishing Company, Flagstaff, AZ, 1987.

Lippmann, John, *Deeper into Diving*, Best Publishing Company, Flagstaff, AZ, 1990.

Mardon, Steve, Ed., "Understanding Circadian Rhythms," *Working Nights*, Premiere Issue, Circadian Information, Cambridge, MA, 1996. Neal, Jan, "Understanding and Equipping for Underwater Vision," *Dive Training Magazine*, June, 2000.

Diving into Darkness

Nevo, Baruch and Stephen Breitstein, *Psychological and Behavioral Aspects of Diving*, Best Publishing Company, Flagstaff, AZ, 1999.

Rossier, Robert N., "Mind and Body: Personal Limits of Fear," *Dive Training Magazine*, Mar. 1998.

Night Dive Planning and Procedures

Francis, John, "Your First Night Dive," *Rodale's Scuba Diving*, Jan./Feb. 1997

Laymon, Lynn, "Night Diving from Shore," *Dive Training Magazine*, Apr. 1997.

Rossier, Robert N., *Dive Like a Pro: 101 Ways to Improve Your Scuba Skills and Safety*, Best Publishing Company, Flagstaff, AZ, 1999.

Rossier, Robert N., "Do It in the Dark: When the Sun Sets, the Ocean Comes Alive," *Dive Training Magazine*, June 1999.

Viders, Hillary, "Night Diving Safety," *Dive Journal*, Mar./Apr. 1997.

Westerfield, Renee, Ed., *The Best of Alert Diver*, Best Publishing Company, Flagstaff, AZ, 1997.

Diving First Aid

Auerbach, Paul S., M.D., *A Medical Guide to Hazardous Marine Life*, Best Publishing Company, Flagstaff, AZ 1997.

Clendenen, Bill, and Dan Orr, "Hazardous Marine Life," *Alert Diver Magazine*, Jan./Feb. 2000.

Burnett, Joseph W., M.D., "Taking the Sting Out of Jellyfish Envenomations," *Alert Diver Magazine*, Mar./Apr. 2000.

Burnett, Joseph W., M.D., "Q & A, Stinging Marine Creatures," *Alert Diver Magazine*, Mar./Apr. 2000.

Mayens, Ed, M.D., "Sea Urchins: A DAN Diving Doc Reminds Us to Beware the Bearers and Wearers of Spines," *Alert Diver Magazine*, Mar./Apr. 2000.

Diving into Darkness

Index

Index

J

Jacks, 27
Jellyfish stings, 75, 97
Jellyfish, 18

K

Kelp, 78, 94
Knife, 55
Krypton, 32

L

Lamp, 30-31, 37
Lanyard, 40, 54, 92
Lead-acid, 37
Lead-acid gel cells, 36
LED (Light Emitting Diode), 33-34
Lens, 34, 46, 49
Lift bag, 5, 52-54, 88, 91
Light signals, 84-85
Lightning, 10, 80
Line, 86, 88
Line reels, 54
Lionfish, 27
Lizardfishes, 26
Lobster, 18, 20
Lost buddy, 90
Lumens, 32-33, 43

M

Magnetic, 38
Magnetic field, 87
Magnetic reed switch, 39
Maintenance, 47, 56
Manta, 18, 25-26
Marker, 4, 30, 41, 75, 82
Marker strobe, 42, 87
Memory, 38
Mental acuity, 15, 62
Mental alertness, 60-63, 70
Mental performance , 62
Mental processes, 66
Mercury, 35
Mergency , 76
Modular lights, 44-45
Mollusca, 21-22
Moray eels, 22

N

National Buoy Data Center, 16
National Weather Service (NWS), 16
Nausea, 91, 99
Navigation, 3-4, 8, 11, 42, 51, 75, 78,
    82-84, 86-88, 94
Nematocysts, 19
Neurotransmitters, 62
Nickel-cadmium (nicad), 36-38
Nickel-metal hydride, 38
Night vision, 64, 84
NOAA, 14-15
NOAA weather, 11
Nudibranchs, 17, 21, 43
Nutrition, 61-62, 66, 76

O

O-ring, 38, 47-48, 50, 56-57
Octopus, 20, 22
Out-of-air, 69-70, 75, 91
Oxygen, 35, 63, 71, 81, 93

P

Palladium, 35
Panic, 89, 92
Parrotfish, 21, 25, 27
Pearlfish, 24
Peripheral vision, 3, 63, 69
Phytoplankton, 18
Pillar corals, 19
Plankton, 2, 17-18, 23, 25, 85
Platyhelminthes, 19
Portuguese man-of-war, 97
Propane, 51
Protein, 62
Puffers, 26

Q

Quartz, 32

R

Range lights, 51, 78, 83
Ray, 25, 27
Rechargeable, 36, 44-45, 56